NEW Y⚬RK

COCKTAILS

AN ELEGANT COLLECTION
OF OVER 100 RECIPES
INSPIRED BY THE BIG APPLE

AMANDA SCHUSTER

CIDER MILL
PRESS

BOOK
PUBLISHERS
KENNEBUNKPORT, MAINE

13-Digit ISBN: 978-1604337297
10-Digit ISBN: 160433729X

This book may be ordered by mail from the publisher. Please include $5.99 for postage and handling. Please support your local bookseller first!

Books published by Cider Mill Press Book Publishers are available at special discounts for bulk purchases in the United States by corporations, institutions, and other organizations. For more information, please contact the publisher.

Cider Mill Press Book Publishers
"Where good books are ready for press"
PO Box 454
12 Spring Street
Kennebunkport, Maine 04046
Visit us on the Web! www.cidermillpress.com

Typography: Avenir, Copperplate, Rennie Mackintosh, Ribbon, Sackers, Warnock

Image Credits: see pages 348-349

Printed in China

4   5   6   7   8   9   0

- Contents -

THE BASICS

WHY NEW YORK COCKTAILS ARE IMPORTANT

"THE TRUE NEW YORKER SECRETLY BELIEVES
THAT PEOPLE LIVING ANYWHERE ELSE HAVE TO BE,
IN SOME SENSE, KIDDING."

—John Updike

One can't tell with the naked eye, but despite the hustle and bustle, New York City is a ghost town. It's a city that is constantly building over itself. Though many original structures are gone, the spirits of its denizens have worked themselves into the cracks and crevices of what came next and continue to influence our lives. Just look at our cocktail culture: Would there even be a need for this book if people such as Harry Johnson, Jerry Thomas and William "The Only William" Schmidt hadn't opened bars in the city and passed on their recipes and techniques? "Improved" cocktails, toddies, Rickeys, juleps, Martinis and, of course, the Manhattan—we're still drinking them. One of the hottest drinks in town right now is a Sherry Cobbler, of all things. A silly experiment like Prohibition couldn't stop us—time certainly won't.

There are lots of tooting horns in this city, but to add to the cacophony: It can be said that people wouldn't be sipping Oaxaca Old

Fashioneds in Cleveland without New York's modern cocktail renaissance. Sasha Petraske, Jack McGarry, Jim Kearns, Julie Reiner, Meaghan Dorman, Audrey Saunders, Dale DeGroff, Joaquín Simó and so many others—these are the neoclassic stars who worked their way up through the bar industry. Now bartenders in places as far as Taipei are mixing their drink recipes.

During Prohibition, we lost many talented barpeople to places where drinking was legal—Paris, Milan, London, Havana and so on. In the time since, those bar cultures boomeranged back into our modern repertoire, where they continue to evolve (hello, BlackTail!). Take Harry's New York in Paris; it's not called "Harry's Chicago Bar," is it? (No offense to Chicago, which has its own impressive bar scene.) Why is one of the most popular bars in Rome called The Jerry Thomas Project? Why do so many bars outside of Brooklyn have "Brooklyn" in their name? It's because the world has an infatuation with New York City culture. Sit in a hotel bar like Bemelmans at the Carlyle, or the Rum House at the Edison, and you might witness someone from Des Moines or Dakar taste their first Manhattan, talking with their bartender about how to make it at home. It's a beautiful thing.

All over town, in every borough, even the most old school joints serve some semblance of a cocktail. And with rent increasing, more of the people who make the really good ones have set up camp in outer neighborhoods. I'd like to think that someone reading this in 2020 will lament that their new bar in Woodlawn didn't make the cut in 2017, or that someone will have *finally* opened a destination cocktail joint near the Staten Island Ferry by the time you read this. A girl can dream. She can certainly drink.

And she's not alone. Let this be your guide to anything cocktail-related in NYC. Where to go, what to drink, how to make it—it's all here. So if you're sipping something right now—and I hope you are—raise your glass to the Big Apple ghosts who have made this city such a wonderful place to drink.

How To Drink Like a New Yorker

Never been to the city but want to blend into the bar scene? Follow these tips and no one will ever guess you're just visiting.

1. The best seat in the house is at the bar.

2. The best time to visit a bar is on a weeknight, an hour or two before closing. (Second only to half an hour after opening.)

3. Know exactly what you want to order when it's time to order, especially in a packed bar.

4. When in doubt, Negroni.

5. The best drink pairing for a burger is a Manhattan, obviously.

6. You're an excellent tipper, especially if you've received a round on the house.

7. Complain incessantly about the oversaturation of cocktail bars in the city as you stand in the packed Dead Rabbit taproom with a Guinness, waiting for your upstairs parlor table.

8. At least three bars are your local spots and at least one of them is nowhere near where you live.

9. You've been Holidayed.

10. "Sorry I'm late. F train."

NEW YORK CITY CLASSIC

AND NEOCLASSIC COCKTAILS

The city is now a veritable mixtape of signature drinks. Some were fixtures before anyone could notice, while others rose to fame alongside the bars and bartenders who created them. While not all of these cocktails can claim to be a native New Yorker, all of these standards have influenced the city's drinking scene in some way—and vice versa. Here are the old standbys, plus some of the new classics that have travelled around the world.

"ONE BELONGS TO NEW YORK INSTANTLY,
ONE BELONGS TO IT AS MUCH IN
FIVE MINUTES AS IN FIVE YEARS."

—*Tom Wolfe*

Martini

A Martini is one of a handful of drinks one can order at almost any bar, from the diviest dive (ingest any garnish at your own risk) to a pillar of swankiness. However, it's also one of the most contentious concoctions. Over the years, the definition of the drink has become a matter of preference rather than fact, though everyone thinks they have the definitive answer. Vodka or gin? Olive or twist? And then there's the million-dollar question: Should a Martini be shaken or stirred?

The answer is yes. To all of it.

One can't just saunter into a bar these days and say, "I'll have a Martini." Further direction is necessary for best results. So rather than share individual recipes, which can be found anywhere these days, here is a rundown of Martini lingo and how to order one.

STRAIGHT UP means the chilled drink is served in a Martini glass without ice, the classic presentation.

ON THE ROCKS is over ice, usually in a stemless glass and rarely seen in the wild.

SERVED DOWN means that it's served in a rocks glass without ice, the Harry's-New-York-Bar-in-Paris way.

CLASSIC/BASIC MARTINI is a 2:1 ratio of gin or vodka (yes, interchangeable here) to dry vermouth, usually garnished with a twist or olive. Served up or on the rocks, though usually up.

PERFECT OR 50/50 MARTINI splits the ratio of base spirit to vermouth evenly, lowering the potential for subsequent mishaps if more than two are consumed. Best served up.

EXTRA DRY MARTINI calls for only a scant amount of vermouth. Most bartenders will make it by swirling some in the glass and discarding before adding chilled spirit. It's often joked that one can simply wave a bottle of vermouth in the direction of the glass and be done.

SHAKEN: Incidentally, this didn't start with James Bond. Watch any movie in the *Thin Man* franchise (based in post-Prohibition 1930s New York, by the way), which stars Myrna Loy and William Powell as Nick and Nora Charles, married madcap sleuths who drink cocktails in almost every scene and keep a mini bar in their bedroom. The Martinis are always shaken. Says Powell as Nick, "The important thing is the rhythm . . .A dry Martini you always shake to waltz time." They were made this way from the beginning. The myth that this method will "bruise" the base spirit is simply not true; it does cloud the base

spirit considerably, but many prefer it this way as it dilutes the drink and keeps it icy cold.

DIRTY MARTINI adds olive brine to any of these recipes, which are of course garnished only with olives.

GIBSON is either a classic, 50/50, or dry Martini served with a cocktail onion instead of twist or olive.

··· NEGRONI ···

Was there really a Count Camillo Negroni, as the most popular legend claims? Or was it another Italian, named Pascal Olivier Count de Negroni, who first ordered an Americano with gin? No one alive knows for sure. Regardless, it's an excellent aperitivo—still one of the most popular to sip almost anywhere in the city, one of the most riffed upon and the best thing to order when a bartender is in the weeds. Whoever invented it certainly deserves a toast.

GARNISH: orange twist

GLASS: rocks

- 1 ounce Campari
- 1 ounce sweet vermouth
- 1 ounce gin

In a rocks glass with ice, combine the ingredients and stir until mixed and chilled. Garnish.

"THIS IS A REALLY FINE INVENTION.
IT HAS THE POWER, RARE WITH DRINKS
AND INDEED WITH ANYTHING ELSE, OF CHEERING YOU UP."

—*Kingsley Amis*

"THE BITTERS ARE EXCELLENT FOR YOUR LIVER, THE GIN IS
BAD FOR YOU. THEY BALANCE EACH OTHER."

—*Orson Welles*

··· BOULEVARDIER ···

This classic cocktail is the rye version of a Negroni. Below is the variation made at Long Island Bar in Brooklyn (see page 256), where it is the house cocktail, with specifications from Toby Cecchini. Careful, this one is pretty high octane!

GARNISH: lemon twist

GLASS: coupe

- 1 ounce Rittenhouse Rye
- 1 ounce Old Overholt Rye
- 1 ounce Campari
- 1 ounce of sweet vermouth, divided ⅓ Carpano Antica and ⅔ Cinzano Rosso

Stir in a mixing glass with ice. Strain into a coupe and garnish.

This drink was invented by Ada Coleman, head bartender of the American Bar at London's Savoy Hotel in the 1920s. It is essentially a Negroni made with Fernet Branca instead of gin. Fernet has been a "bartender's handshake" shot in the city for several years, and this classic has regained status as a standard order for many folks of the bitter persuasion. It's one of those miracle cocktails that shouldn't work, but somehow does.

GLASS: coupe
GARNISH: orange twist

- 1½ ounces gin
- 1 ounce sweet vermouth
- 2 dashes Fernet Branca liqueur

1. Stir all ingredients in a mixing glass with ice. Strain into the coupe.

2. Express the peel into the glass and then arrange it over the surface of the drink.

Spotlight: Dale DeGroff

We likely wouldn't be discussing New York cocktails if it weren't for the man known as King Cocktail, who in many ways changed the way we drink. When Dale DeGroff moved to the city in 1969 it was, as he puts it, the end of one era and the beginning of another, with Swing Street giving way to CBGB. "It was a beer and highball, rum and Tab town, then—Chardonnay, a Mimosa or Bloody Mary, maybe you could order a breeze [Seabreeze, etc.] or something made with fake sour mix." However, it was true then as it is now that "adopting a neighborhood bar was to become part of an extended family."

A part-time actor, DeGroff began working in the restaurant industry to make a living before he eventually landed as head bartender at

the second revamp (we are currently in our third as of press time) of the Rainbow Room in the '80s. Its owner, restaurateur Joe Baum of Restaurant Associates, wanted a classic cocktail menu for the space, which was to have 34 bartenders on staff. He handed DeGroff a copy of Jerry Thomas' *Bartenders Manual* and told him to get busy making drinks. There were simply no other references, and "the only real cocktail menus in town were at the Waldorf, Bull and Bear and the Plaza." People began paying attention to the Rainbow Room, which received terrific publicity for its classic concoctions made with fresh juices and quality spirits. DeGroff was at the forefront of this rediscovered ideology for cocktail service—that a good drink is an experience, beginning with the bartender interaction and ending with how the drink tastes and what mood it sets. Things were really changing, he says, "when I went to a bar downtown and saw a Between the Sheets [a Prohibition-era drink] on a cocktail menu."

After the Rainbow Room closed, DeGroff began working in and consulting on other bars in the city (Balthazar, Pravda, Pastis, etc.), mentoring the likes of Audrey Saunders, Julie Reiner and countless others before finally writing his first book, *The Craft of the Cocktail,* in 2002. ("I guess I was an expert by then," he says.) He is a co-founder of bartender training program Beverage Alcohol Resource (BAR) with David Wondrich, Doug Frost, F. Paul Paccult, Andy Seymour and Steve Olson, and co-founder of the Museum of the American Cocktail in New Orleans. His talented wife Jill has also made a name for herself as a self-styled Saloon Artist. It is considered one of the highest honors in the cocktail industry to be rendered in one of Jill's caricatures.

This is a Peacock Alley favorite. Oddly enough, it is not named for the Scottish bard (although it makes a fine Burns Night cocktail), but rather a regular guest at the Old Waldorf-Astoria Bar who worked for the Robert Burns Cigar Company. This is the Harry Craddock variation, as interpreted by Frank Caiafa, in his 2016 update of *The Waldorf Astoria Bar Book*.

GLASS: coupe
GARNISH: lemon twist

- 2 ounces Spencerfield Sheep Dip or Johnnie Walker Black
- 1 ounce Dolin sweet vermouth
- ¼ ounce Bénédictine liqueur
- 1 dash Regan's Orange Bitters No. 6

Add all ingredients to a mixing glass with ice and stir for 30 seconds. Strain into chilled coupe and garnish.

··· THE BRONX COCKTAIL ···

Are there cocktails in the Bronx? That's like asking if there is a Fourth of July in England. They exist, but there are no fireworks. This cocktail is probably the most famous Bronx-adjacent cocktail; invented around the same time as the Brooklyn, it has the distinction, according to author Philip Greene, of being the preferred drink of Bill Wilson—yes, the founder of Alcoholics Anonymous. This is bartender Frank Caiafa's recipe for the historic Peacock Alley bar at the Waldorf Astoria Hotel. Sadly, the bar has closed, but you can still make one at home!

GARNISH: none

GLASS: coupe or Martini

- 1½ ounces London dry gin (bar uses Beafeater)
- ½ ounce sweet vermouth (bar uses Cinzano)
- ½ ounce extra dry vermouth (bar uses Noilly Prat)
- 1 ounce fresh orange juice
- 1 dash Regan's Orange Bitters No. 6 (recipe states this is optional, but it's better this way)

Shake all ingredients with ice. Strain into a chilled cocktail glass (doublestrain if the juice is very pulpy).

—Cosmopolitan—

T here has been some controversy over the years as to the Cosmopolitan's rightful inventor, but most claims are unfounded. In fact, there are two versions of the Cosmopolitan, but the one that rose to fame during the *Sex in the City* era has become the default. Here are the facts, according to the person who can claim to be the drink's rightful creator, Toby Cecchini:

• There's a version made from rail vodka, Rose's lime and grenadine that was popular in San Francisco nightclubs in the 1970s and '80s. This is different, changing up the "red" component and the lime.

• It was born in the autumn of 1988 at the nightspot Odeon in New York City, when then-bartender Cecchini was introduced to a new vodka product called Absolut Citron (The flavor is *in* the vodka! What a concept!), and mixed up something fun for the waitresses who worked there.

• This version could not have existed in 1985 in Miami, where someone else has laid claim to the recipe. Absolut Citron had not even been conceived as a product yet.

• Regulars at the bar, most famously Madonna and her gal pal Sandra Bernhard, ordered the drink by yelling, "Boyfriend! Give us those pink drinks!"

• 10 years later it was popularized on *Sex and the City*.

• Cecchini has never seen an episode of the series.

Many have attempted to elevate this recipe by using more upscale vodka or gin and organic, unsweetened cranberry, but it just doesn't taste right unless made the following way. Don't fix what ain't broke.

GARNISH: lemon twist (not orange, not lime, not flaming)

GLASS: Martini

- 1½ ounces Absolut Citron
- ¾ ounce fresh lime juice
- ¾ ounce Cointreau
- ¾ ounce Ocean Spray Cranberry juice cocktail

Shake all ingredients with ice. Strain into glass. Garnish.

··· ROME WITH A VIEW ···

Need to switch to something low-alcohol but still want a drink? Most cocktail bartenders keep this one in their repertoire for just such a situation. It is attributed to Michael (Micky) McIlroy from Attaboy, though variations abound. This is my preferred spec, with less acid than the original formula, though if you want more juice just increase the quantities to 1 ounce of lime juice and ¾ ounce of syrup.

◆◆

GARNISH: orange wheel, lime twist,
lemon wheel, basically something citrus
GLASS: Collins

- 1 ounce Campari
- 1 ounce dry vermouth
- ½ ounce lime juice
- ¼ ounce simple syrup
- soda water

1. Add all ingredients except soda to a cocktail shaker and shake with ice. Strain into an ice-filled Collins glass.

2. Top with soda water. Garnish.

··· PENICILLIN ···

This modern classic is attributed to Sam Ross at Little Branch and Attaboy, but it has traveled the world over. This is a fun drink to make for people who say they don't like smokiness or ginger, or both. Somehow the flavor combination is so soothing (hence the name), you can't get mad at it. Ross' recipe calls for a separate ginger syrup made with fresh ginger juice. If you have the means, go for it. For the home bartender, I find making honey syrup with a big hunk of ginger will also do the trick. At Ross and Michael McIlroy's Brooklyn bar Diamond Reef, they serve a frozen version: the Penichillin.

GARNISH: lemon twist (optional)
GLASS: rocks/Old Fashioned

- 2 ounces blended Scotch (one that is not smoky, like Compass Box Asyla, regular Famous Grouse or Monkey Shoulder)
- ¾ ounce fresh lemon juice
- ¾ ounce honey-ginger syrup (add 2 inches of sliced fresh ginger while making standard 1:1 honey syrup)
- ¼ ounce smoky Islay Scotch (I use Compass Box Peat Monster, Laphroaig or Lagavulin)

1. Shake all ingredients except the smoky Scotch with ice. Strain over ice into a rocks glass.

2. Delicately poor the smoky Scotch over the back of a barspoon to float it over the drink. Garnish if desired.

··· THE CLOVER CLUB COCKTAIL ···

The Clover Club is one of the first bars on the modern cocktail scene in Brooklyn. Here is owner Julie Reiner's version for the classic cocktail that bears its name, which also appears in her book *The Craft of the Cocktail Party*. As she puts it, "it is a gin drink for people who hate gin, at turns fruity and dry." The original Clover Club for gentlemen was in the Bellvue-Stratford Hotel in Philadelphia, and it was a haven for writers and intellectuals who held roasts there. "I find it humorous that the original Clover Club was a real boys' club, and that my Clover Club is run by three women. I like to think we are snarky and bawdy enough to have held our own with those boys."

GARNISH: 2 raspberries on a cocktail pick

GLASS: coupe

- 1½ ounces dry gin
- ½ dry vermouth
- ½ ounce lemon juice
- ½ ounce raspberry syrup (or muddle 5 raspberries in ½ ounce simple syrup)
- ½ ounce egg white (about half the white of one egg)

1. Combine all ingredients in a shaker and dry shake for about 20 seconds.

2. Add ice and shake until chilled.

3. Strain into a coupe and spear the berries on a pick to lay across the rim of the glass.

According to cocktail historian David Wondrich (see page 58), this cocktail wasn't actually born in New York, but Chicago (hopefully that makes up for my comment in the intro). Basically an egg white–less whiskey sour with a dash of red wine, this was a popular drink at city speakeasies during Prohibition, where it was used to mask flavors of inferior whiskey. As an added bonus, it's also a great way to use up open wine. This version, from Garrett Smith, proprietor of Cherry Point in Brooklyn, combines smoky blended Scotch with Italian wine to match the smoky meats from the restaurant's kitchen (and give it an "old man bar" vibe). You can sub out the Scotch for bourbon, rye or other blended Scotch and still have a terrific drink.

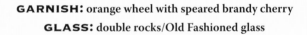

GARNISH: orange wheel with speared brandy cherry
GLASS: double rocks/Old Fashioned glass

- 2 ounces Famous Grouse Smokey Black Scotch (formerly known as Black Grouse)
- ¾ ounce simple syrup
- ¾ ounce fresh lemon juice
- ¼ ounce dry red wine (bar uses Dolcetto d'Alba)

1. Shake all ingredients except wine in a mixing tin with ice. Strain into glass over ice.

2. Gently pour the wine over the back of a barspoon to float over the drink. Garnish with a pick over the drink.

These have come a long way since the dark days following Prohibition, when almost every bar in town would make them with artificial sour mix. These days, fresh juice is thankfully the norm. Fun fact: this cocktail is hands-down the best accompaniment to barbecue, wings with a tangy sauce or Chinese takeout. This version comes courtesy of Derrick Turner, head bartender at Harding's.

GARNISH: 1 dash Peychaud's Bitters or Angostura bitters, cherry and/or orange slice

GLASS: coupe or rocks glass

- 2 ounces rye or bourbon whiskey (bar uses Whistle Pig rye)
- 1 ounce fresh lemon juice
- ½ ounce simple syrup
- 1 egg white

1. Add all ingredients to mixing tin. Dry shake for 15 to 20 seconds.

2. Open tin and add ice to mixture. Shake hard for 10 seconds. Double strain into a large coupe or rocks glass.

3. Add dash of bitters on top of the cocktail and swirl into the froth. Garnish with cherry or orange slice, or combine the two on a toothpick placed over the drink.

··· GIN-GIN MULE ···

This gingery cocktail was created by Audrey Saunders for Pegu Club (see page 42) as a gateway gin drink for vodka lovers. Not only did it succeed, it inspired many variations around the world. Here is the recipe with her very own specs, including her recipe for ginger beer.

GLASS: 10-ounce highball

GARNISH: mint sprig, lime wheel and candied ginger;
serve with long straws

- ¾ ounce fresh lime juice
- 1 ounce simple syrup
- 2 mint sprigs (1 for muddling; 1 for garnish)
- 1 ounce homemade ginger beer (see page 36)
- 1 ¾ ounce Tanqueray Classic Gin

1. Measure lime juice, simple syrup and mint into a mixing glass. Muddle well.

2. Add gin, ginger beer, and ice. Shake well, and strain into a highball glass. Garnish and add straw.

—Audrey Saunders'—
Ginger Beer

Says Saunders: "The trick is the homemade ginger beer . . . because the store-bought stuff has a peppery (more than gingery) profile—and many times insipid." Still, "if you've absolutely got to go there and use the canned stuff, then reduce the simple syrup in the drink down to ½ ounce (or less, depending on how sweet the canned stuff is)."

LARGE BATCH (1 GALLON)

- 1 pound ginger root, minced
- 1 gallon water
- 4 ounces light brown sugar (or 6 ounces light agave syrup)
- 2 ounce fresh lime juice

1. Add water to a pot and bring to a boil.

2. Break-up ginger root into smaller pieces, and place in a food processor. Add a cup of the boiling water to make processing easier. Process until the mixture is almost mulch-like.

3. After you've minced the ginger, add it back into the boiling water. Shut off heat. Stir well, then cover for 1 hour.

4. Strain through a fine chinois or cheesecloth, then add the lime juice and light brown sugar. Let cool.

5. Transfer into bottled containers and store in the refrigerator.

TIP. While you are straining the ginger, take a spoon or ladle and firmly press down on the ginger to extract the flavor. The strongest part of the ginger essence hides in there, and needs to be pressed out manually. Its appearance will be cloudy—don't worry, that's natural.

SMALL BATCH—1 CUP

- 1 cup water
- 2 tablespoons fresh ginger, finely grated
- ½ teaspoon fresh lime juice
- 1 teaspoon light brown sugar

Follow the same directions for the large batch, but grate the ginger instead of using the food processor.

··· OAXACA OLD FASHIONED ···

Phil Ward created this drink while working at Death & Co, and it became one of his signature cocktails when he opened his agave-centric bar Mayahuel. Combining tequila reposado and mezcal, this drink offers a nice earthy balance with a touch of sweetness.

❖

GARNISH: flamed orange twist

GLASS: Old Fashioned/rocks

- 1½ ounces El Tesoro tequila reposado
- ½ ounce Del Maguey San Luis Del Rio mezcal
- 2 dashes Angostura bitters
- 1 barspoon agave nectar

1. Combine all the ingredients except the orange twist in an Old Fashioned glass with one large ice cube. Stir until chilled.

2. Top with a flamed orange twist and serve.

MAYAHUEL
304 East 6th Street
New York, NY 10003
(212) 253-5888
mayahuelny.com
reservations recommended

Named for the divine protector of the maguey plant in Mexico, Mayahuel bar was opened in 2009 by former Death & Co bartender Phil Ward. Ward set out to champion agave spirits as a sophisticated cocktail base—something other than a vehicle for Margaritas, although those are great too. The bar has a considerable menu of snacks, small plates, tacos and other bites as well.

··· TRINIDAD SOUR ···

The cocktail world did a double take when Giuseppe González first brought this drink into the limelight. There's *how* much Ango in this? How can that be right? It's right—taste and you'll understand.

◆◆◆

GARNISH: none

GLASS: coupe

- 1½ ounces Angostura bitters
- ½ ounce rye
- ¾ ounce lemon juice
- 1 ounce orgeat

Shake all ingredients with ice. Strain into coupe.

··· HAITIAN DIVORCE ···

This sherry-focused cocktail by Tom Richter (see page 154) now resides at Dear Irving, but was created at the Beagle (see page 244) and is replicated at many bars across the city.

❖

GARNISH: orange and lime twists
GLASS: double Old Fashioned/rocks

- 1½ ounces Barbancourt 8 year rum
- ¾ ounce del Maguey Vida mezcal
- ½ ounce Pedro Ximenez sherry
- 2 dashes Angostura bitters

Place all ingredients in the rocks glass—preferably with large ice, though smaller cubes will work—and stir until combined and chilled. Garnish.

— *Spotlight:* —
Audrey Saunders and Pegu Club

77 West Houston Street
New York, NY 10012
(212) 473-7348
peguclub.com

When it opened in 2005, Pegu Club brought the masses a new way to imbibe cocktails. It gracefully situated itself between the opulence of an upscale New York venue—like Rainbow Room, where Saunders trained under Dale DeGroff—and the nonchalance of a proper saloon. Though its entrance is discreet, it's not a speakeasy, and though it is cavernous, ornately detailed and sparsely lit, it is not a nightclub. Only those with impeccable service ability and cocktail knowledge work behind the bar, and it's seen an impressive roster over the years—Phil Ward, Toby Maloney, Jim Kearns, Del Pedro, St. John Frizell, Giuseppe González and Kenta Goto, to name a few.

This SoHo cocktail oasis has endured because, after all this time, its accessible sophistication sets it apart from an oversaturated bar scene. Below, Saunders shares some insight into her approach.

On opening Pegu Club in the earlier days SoHo cocktails: "I spent a number of treasured years amassing an expert craft cocktail education and learning about service etiquette while working alongside Dale DeGroff, whom I consider an outstanding mentor. As I progressed into the role of Beverage Director of Bemelmans Bar at The Carlyle Hotel in 2001, I was given carte blanche to implement its beverage programs, and at the same time was able to delve deeper into the finer points of 5-star operations and service standards. The enriching combination of both experiences equipped me with the tools and confidence necessary to be able to stand on my own, and I view them as invaluable. Pegu Club was a natural extension of both."

On the bar's aesthetic: "The original Pegu Club was a British officer's club in Rangoon in the late 1800s, and its house cocktail was a bittered sour that utilized London Dry gin. Much of my work was gin-based leading up to the opening, and at that same time, it was countercurrent to a bar culture which mostly offered fruity vodka and rum drinks. My intent in naming the bar 'Pegu Club' was to send a message to the cocktail subculture (at that time) that this would be a civilized place to drink—and given the complexity of its brisk, dry house cocktail, that I would also be resurrecting gin and other forgotten classics as its strength."

On choosing such stellar bartenders before they'd made their mark: "Before I opened Pegu, there already existed a fairly small community of like-minded craft-bartenders, and we all knew each other fairly well. As I shared my ideas for Pegu with them, they shared back, and many showed great interest. Yet while knowing how to make a good drink is important, at the end of the day it's the level of hospitality you offer your guests that keeps them coming back. I strive for both. While I can certainly teach a person how to bartend, I cannot teach them to have a warm personality—that has to come from within. I look for individuals with a flicker in their eyes, who enjoy giving to others, who have a passion for learning and a strong commitment to excellence. These are qualities that I am able to innately sense right out of the gate. When I look back on it, it was more about bringing their individual personalities together and forming a great rock band that jammed well together."

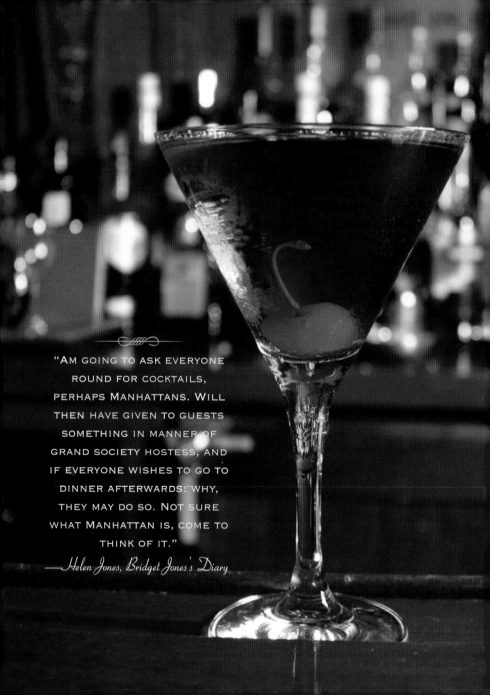

"AM GOING TO ASK EVERYONE
ROUND FOR COCKTAILS,
PERHAPS MANHATTANS. WILL
THEN HAVE GIVEN TO GUESTS
SOMETHING IN MANNER OF
GRAND SOCIETY HOSTESS, AND
IF EVERYONE WISHES TO GO TO
DINNER AFTERWARDS: WHY,
THEY MAY DO SO. NOT SURE
WHAT MANHATTAN IS, COME TO
THINK OF IT."

—Helen Jones, Bridget Jones's Diary

THE MANHATTAN

The most iconic of all New York City cocktails—the one that has inspired the most variations, the most declarations of love, the most false claims about its origins—is the Manhattan. Author Philip Greene published a whole book about it in 2016, titled *The Manhattan: The Story of the First Modern Cocktail.* He attempts to solve the mystery of who invented the drink once and for all, but comes up with two conclusions, either of which could be correct: that it was created for a guest at a reception at the Manhattan Club in the mid 1870s, or that bartender George Black came up with it at the Manhattan Inn around the same time. The unsatisfying truth is that it could have been anyone, really; it's not as though old bartenders went out of their way to publish articles about their drinks, as they do now. Regardless, by the early 1880s, the cocktail had made the rounds and everyone loved it. Let's just say it was almost certainly born in New York City and leave it at that. Here's the classic recipe, plus a few familiar and not-so-familiar variations.

··· MANHATTAN ···

GARNISH: lemon twist or cherry*
GLASS: coupe or Martini

- **2 ounces rye whiskey****
- **1 ounce sweet vermouth**
- **2 dashes Angostura bitters**

Stir all ingredients with ice.*** Strain into glass. Garnish.

> * While lemon is a perfectly acceptable garnish, I personally think the Manhattan is the ultimate vessel for a well made cocktail cherry. Why deny yourself one of life's great treats?
>
> ** A real Manhattan is made with rye. Sure, you could use bourbon, another delicious option. But if you're going for authenticity, start with rye. From there, you can tinker with whiskey, bitters and garnishes to your heart's desire.
>
> ***Technically, it's not *wrong* to shake a Manhattan. For all you purists ready to quote *Thin Man* lines at me, I admit it—many early recipes call for shaking your mix, rather than stirring. It's not undrinkable, but for my money, a brown, cloudy, cold soup with a frothy pink layer does not a Manhattan make.

··· PERFECT MANHATTAN ···

Same recipe and method, only divide the vermouth into ½ an ounce of sweet (red) and ½ an ounce of dry (white). This is how I usually order it, especially in an establishment with good vermouth.

··· THE BROOKLYN ···

This spinoff was first published in the early 20th century, though not by its inventor. Again, bartenders weren't as concerned with bragging rights back then. The star ingredient, Amer Picon, is very hard to come by in the states, but it can be found. The internet has lots of advice on how to cheat the ingredient, but it's as reliable as diagnosing Rocky Mountain spotted fever with an app. If you can get your hands on some, buy at least two bottles and make this fantastic drink with only that ingredient. If not, Bigallet China-China Amer is a decent substitute.

GARNISH: none, officially

GLASS: coupe

- 1½ ounces rye whiskey (bonded, preferably)
- 1½ ounces dry vermouth
- ½ tsp (barspoon) maraschino liqueur
- ½ tsp (barspoon) Amer Picon

Stir all ingredients with ice (most recipes note the ice is cracked). Strain into coupe. There is no official garnish, but it's very nice with a cherry to match the cherry liqueur, if you so choose.

At this famous West Village bar, the house Manhattan gets a refreshing tinge of orange from Grand Marnier.

❖

GARNISH: lemon twist

GLASS: cocktail coupe

- 1½ ounces Rittenhouse Rye Whiskey
- 1¾ ounces Cocchi Sweet Vermouth
- ½ ounce Grand Marnier
- 3 dashes of Angostura bitters

1. Pour the whiskey, vermouth, liqueur, and bitters into a mixing glass. Add large cold ice cubes and stir for 40 revolutions.

2. Strain into a chilled cocktail glass. Garnish with a lemon twist.

··· MARTINEZ ···

Yes, fine, technically this is a Martini variation. It's the predecessor to the Martini, to be precise. But think about it: boozy base, something "red," bitters—it's a vermouth-forward gin Manhattan, right? Right? Oh, just make it and drink it.

GARNISH: lemon twist

GLASS: coupe (Nick Nora–sized is best since this is a small aperitif)

- 2 ounces sweet vermouth
- 1 ounce Old Tom gin
- 1 scant barspoon maraschino liqueur
- 2 dashes Angostura bitters (Jerry Thomas' 1887 recipe calls for Bokers)

Stir all ingredients with ice. Strain into the glass. Garnish.

··· BLOOD, LUST AND DIAMONDS ···

GARNISH: cherry

GLASS: coupe

- 2 ounces rye
- ¾ ounce Bonal
- ½ ounce Cognac
- 1 dash Angostura
- 1 dash Peychaud's
- 1 dash amaretto

Stir all ingredients with ice. Strain into the glass. Garnish

"THIS COMES FROM A QUOTE BY JACOBEAN DRAMATIST JOHN WEBSTER (C. 1580—C. 1634),'WHETHER WE FALL BY AMBITION, BLOOD, OR LUST, LIKE DIAMONDS, WE ARE CUT WITH OUR OWN DUST.'"

—*Bryan Teoh, creator*

Here's my rum Manhattan variation that switches out the rye with dark rum. With the lime twist, it reminds me of the tiki drink Jet Pilot without the juice!

GARNISH: lime twist

GLASS: coupe

- 1½ ounces aged dark rum (7—12 years)
- ½ ounce dry vermouth
- ½ ounce Bigallet China-China
- 2 dashes chocolate or mole bitters

1. Stir all ingredients with ice. Strain into the glass.

2. Express lime over the drink by wiping the rim peel side–down and drop the lime into the drink.

··· VIEUX CARRÉ (THE OLD QUARTER) ···

This is a Manhattan with a Southern accent, born in New Orleans in the 1930s. One of my best friends always orders it in New York because he likes both Cognac and rye. While it's not quite as sweet as a Manhattan, it's also not as strong because it's on the rocks. Even better, it's easy to remember the measurements because they're mostly equal parts. Everybody wins.

GARNISH: lemon twist

GLASS: Old Fashioned

- ¾ ounce rye
- ¾ ounce cognac
- ¾ ounce sweet vermouth
- 1 barspoon Bénédictine liqueur
- 1 dash Peychaud's bitters
- 1 dash Angostura bitters

Stir all ingredients with ice. Strain into an Old Fashioned glass over fresh ice.

Audrey Saunders' delicious recipe at Pegu Club uses Cynar Italian artichoke bitters as a tribute to its bordering neighborhood. This also adds a dry, yet rich, dimension to the classic. Saunders insists that the ingredients be brand-specific for best results.

GLASS: Nick & Nora

GARNISH: 2 Luxardo Cherries

- **2 ounces Rittenhouse Rye**
- **½ ounce Cynar**
- **¾ ounce Martini & Rossi Sweet Vermouth**

Measure all the ingredients into a mixing glass. Fill with ice, stir well, and strain into a chilled cocktail glass.

The Manhattan is often considered a fall or winter drink, but Mike Vacheresse of Brooklyn's Travel Bar serves this light, citrusy take when the weather heats up. Be careful: It's a little too easy to sip this one.

GARNISH: lemon twist

GLASS: coupe

- 2 ounces Old Overholt rye
- 1 ounce Dubonnet Rouge
- 3 dashes Regan's No. 6 bitters

Stir all ingredients with ice. Strain into glass. Garnish.

Another Vacheresse Travel Bar original, the smoke comes from Amaro Sfumato, a key ingredient that imparts a dramatic, cloudy appearance.

GARNISH: cherry or orange twist

GLASS: coupe

- 2 ounce Old Overhold rye
- ¾ ounce Amaro Sfumato
- 2 dashes Regan's Orange bitters No. 6

Stir all ingredients with ice. Strain into glass. Garnish.

··· SFORZANDO ···

This is an even smokier variation, which was created by bartender Eryn Reece during her tenure at Death & Co.

GARNISH: orange twist

GLASS: coupe

- 1 ounce Rittenhouse Rye (bonded)
- ¾ ounce Del Maguey Chichicapa Mezcal
- ½ ounce Bénédictine liqueur
- ½ ounce Dolin Dry Vermouth
- 2 dashes Bitterman's Mole Bitters

Stir all ingredients with ice and strain into glass. Garnish.

Spotlight: David Wondrich

Writer and historian David Wondrich has become one of the go-to consultants when you want to party like it's 1899. Need to recreate a lost spirit? Find out who was behind the stick at the long-gone City Hotel? Learn the proper measurements for an old recipe that vaguely recommends using a "pony" of an ingredient? Call Dave.

Wondrich says his career began through the "law of unintended consequences." Really, all he and his wife wanted was to find a good drink. "We liked our bars, but we just wanted them to make better cocktails." It wasn't easy. One had to know where they were, and which bar made what drink well. After a day at the Met, for example, go to Bemelmans for the Stinger or find the good bartender at Joe Allen in the theater district, or visit Del Pedro at Grange Hall (see page 243). Per Wondrich, it was a matter of, "Hey! The guy here can make a Sidecar! This guy over here makes a Manhattan!. . .it's not as though we were dying of thirst. Everyone could make a decent Martini. Although even elegant bars would make shit drinks."

Part of the problem is what Wondrich refers to as the "dumbing down" of drinks. Spirits came with terrible recipe cards and venues would make those drinks as an incentive to get better deals on the products. "Drinks like the Fuzzy Navel were invented in a corporate board room."

Cut to the late 1990s and the rise of the Internet. Wondrich found himself aligning with likeminded "cocktail geeks" like Robert Hess, who had the DrinkBoy cocktail site—a favorite forum for posting cocktail findings that attracted readers like Audrey Saunders and Ted Haigh. At the time, Wondrich was an English professor and music writer for *Esquire*. The writing pivoted toward cocktails, and because it was way more fun, cocktail writing took over.

The rest is history. Lots of history. His books include *Imbibe!* and *Punch*, and he's written countless columns for *Esquire*, *Eater* and *Imbibe*, among many others. He is now a weekly columnist for the *Daily Beast* while he compiles an encyclopedia of drink during what passes for his spare time. He has consulted on quite a few spirits projects, including Dry Curaçao and O.F.T.D. Rum for Pierre Ferrand/Plantation, The Emerald Whiskey for Ransom Spirits and Chief Gowanus for NY Distilling (see page 334). Yes, much has changed since the tumbleweed era of New York City drinking: "It's almost weirder now to order a Martini in a dive bar."

Essential Cocktails and Where to Drink Them

To paraphrase Frank Sinatra in *New York, New York:* if you can make it there, you can make it anywhere. These are the cocktails that are best when made and enjoyed right where they are.

CLOVER CLUB, CLOVER CLUB No, it was not created *for* the bar, as many would assume (see page 98). Nonetheless, Julie Reiner's variation is in its proper new home.

NAKED AND FAMOUS, DEATH & CO This bar is one of the reasons New York became a cocktail town again, and this drink by Joaquín Simó is one of the ways New Yorkers found their way to mezcal (see page 118).

GARIBALDI CAFFÉ, DANTE Even people who say they don't like orange juice cocktails love this glass of fluffy sunshine (see page 254).

BOULEVARDIER, COSMOPOLITAN, LONG ISLAND BAR The Boulevardier, essentially a rye Negroni, has been a perennial favorite since Long Island Bar opened 2014. Its owner, Toby Cecchini, is the man credited with inventing the Cosmopolitan (see page 27). He'll make you one if you ask nicely—but probably not until you've had at least a Boulevardier first (see page 18).

MARTINI, '21' CLUB Although their bar is well stocked with essentials for a wide variety of drinks, and their signature is a Southside (see page 83), it seems almost wrong to order anything else here. This is where writer Robert Benchley famously said, "Why don't you get out of that wet coat and into a dry Martini?"

SNAPPER KING COLE, BAR AT THE ST. REGIS New York's first version of the Bloody Mary (brought to us by Ferdinand Petiot of Harry's New Bar in 1921) is the Snapper; this hotel bar, with its glorious mural by Maxfield Parrish, is where it originated.

GIN-GIN MULE, PEGU CLUB This modern classic has made the rounds, but if you want to drink it with homemade ginger beer, get it at the source (see page 35).

MANHATTAN, KEEN'S OR BEMELMANS BAR AT THE CARLYLE (TIE) There is no question that a Manhattan is the best companion to a fine steak, so it's no surprise that one of the best places to drink one is at Keen's, one of the city's most revered steak houses. Why Bemelmans too? At first glance, it may seem like just another overpriced cocktail at a swanky hotel bar. However, this one arrives in a standard Martini glass along with a mini decanter of nearly another drink's worth on ice. It also comes with a tray of free (what my mother refers to as "gratuitous") bar snacks, which includes cheese straws, nuts and chips. In cocktail math, that $20+ drink just saved you at least $15 elsewhere.

IRISH COFFEE, DEAD RABBIT This is one of the only cocktails available on every floor of the multi-level tavern, and truly one of the best iterations ever created (see page 221).

TIA MIA, LEYENDA This rummy, tropical concoction with the flower garnish was the first drink created for Leyenda. Sip it in summertime for refreshment; drink it in winter when you've forgotten what summer feels like (see page 103).

OAXACA OLD FASHIONED, MAYAHUEL The game-changing, agave-based drink was created by Phil Ward at Death & Co and became one of his signature cocktails when he opened his own bar (see page 38).

PENICILLIN, ATTABOY Hate ginger? Hate smoky Scotch? Sam Ross' comforting creation might change your mind (see page 29).

SAKURA MARTINI, BAR GOTO A drink with a fresh cherry blossom in the glass—how can you not smile as you sip it? (see page 165)

SMOKY OLD FASHIONED, AMOR Y AMARGO This is the "animal style" of AyA. "It's the most ordered drink at the bar and it's not even on the menu," says Sother Teague.

IMPROVED PIÑA COLADA, SUFFOLK ARMS At this Giuseppe González–owned bar, this variation of the popular blender-bar classic takes the "guilt" out of "guilty pleasure." (See page 193)

PEACE TREATY, DEAR IRVING, THE BENNET, RAINES LAW ROOM A sherry-focused cocktail from Tom Richter, can be ordered these three sister bars—all united under one cocktail. If only world peace were this simple (or delicious). (See page 155)

GUN METAL BLUE, PORCHLIGHT Blue drinks are back, and this breakout Instagram star is partially to blame. One taste, though, and all is forgiven. (See page 167)

PRE AND PRO-HIBITION

It is important to recognize that this modern age of cocktails would be inconceivable without what came before. After all, Dale DeGroff wouldn't have been steered toward a copy of Jerry Thomas' *Bartender's Guide*, a book written over a century before his time, had its contents no longer been relevant. Sure, most of the book's instructions are dated and vague—for instance, how much exactly is a "wineglass" of brandy? And who knows how to make gum syrup? But the recipes still work; the books written by 19th and early 20th–century bartenders, many of whom lived in New York City, contain the first iterations of what became cocktail canon. They made the modern classics possible, and "cocktail geeks" have been collecting and sharing them for good reason.

Let's do a little time traveling.

Pre-Prohibition Cocktails

New York City has always been cool. Celebrity bartenders worked here even before the 20th century began! With the today's cocktail renaissance, versions of their recipes continue to spill into glasses around the city, even though their bars have been built over several times. Here are just a few of the time-honored classics.

··· THE IMPROVED COCKTAIL ···

Prior to the 1870s, the word "cocktail" referred specifically to one type of drink—a combination of base spirit, sugar, bitters and water. Bartender Jerry Thomas is credited with building on this formula, and the first recipes for "improved" versions of cocktails appeared in the second edition of his seminal book, *The Bartenders Guide: How to Mix Drinks, or The Bon Vivant's Companion*. For the Improved Brandy Cocktail, he adds maraschino cherry liqueur, absinthe and a lemon twist—creating a a template for cocktails that use different base spirits.

❖

GARNISH: lemon peel
GLASS: rocks

- **2 ounces spirit of choice (gin, bourbon, rye or brandy)**
- **¼ ounce simple syrup (note: original recipe calls for gum syrup)**
- **2 dashes (equivalent to a barspoon) of Maraschino liqueur such as Luxardo**
- **1 dash Absinthe**
- **2 dashes bitters**

1. In a rocks glass, stir the syrup with the maraschino, bitters and absinthe.

2. Add the base spirit of choice and stir to combine.

3. Add ice, preferably one large cube and stir to chill.

4. Wipe the lemon peel skin side–down around the rim of the glass, express the oils into the glass and drop into the drink.

This one comes from William Schmidt, known as "The Only William," who ran a bar at the base of the Brooklyn Bridge in the late 1800s. For a good 16 years or so, following an article in the *New York Sun*, The Only William was the most famous bartender in the world. His 1891 book, *The Flowing Punch Bowl: When and What To Drink* (the first edition can be viewed for free at euvslibrary.com), contains many multi-ingredient recipes calling for ingredients like crème de roses, which even now seem a little fussy. However, this relatively easy, punch-like refresher really hits the spot on a hot day. His recipe was built in glass, but it's better when the ingredients are shaken and then strained in.

GARNISH: lemon wheel, straw

GLASS: Collins or Julep cup

- 2 ounces Cognac VSOP
- 1 ounce Grand Marnier liqueur
- juice of half a lemon
- ½ ounce rich simple syrup
- 1 dash orange bitters
- seltzer or club soda

1. Shake all ingredients well with ice.

2. Strain into an ice-filled glass (crushed ice is best, but regular cubes get the job done). Garnish and sip through straw.

··· THE APPLE TODDY ···

After pie, toddies used to be the most American apple-related treat. Bartender Orsamus Willard was an early master of the drink during his stint at the City Hotel around 1815, and it was still popular decades later when Jerry Thomas tweaked the recipe for the 1862 *Bartenders Guide*.

GARNISH: grated nutmeg

GLASS: glass mug

- 1 teaspoon simple syrup (original wording is "sugar dissolved in water")
- 1 wine glass of cider brandy (applejack)
- ½ of a baked apple
- boiling water

1. Add all ingredients to a glass mug. Fill with boiling water and stir to combine.

2. Grate the nutmeg over the drink and serve.

··· THE BIJOU COCKTAIL ···

This vermouth-forward gin cocktail (the name is French for "jewel") first appeared in the 1900 edition of Harry Johnson's *Bartenders Manual*. It appeared around the same time he opened his last bar, the Endymion at 352 West 117th Street, per drink historians Jared Brown and Anistatia Miller in their book *The Deans of Drink*. Johnson's version calls for equal parts of the spirits, but today most bartenders increase the amount of gin to make it slightly drier.

❖

GARNISH: lemon peel or cherry

GLASS: coupe

- 1½ ounce dry gin (Johnson would have used Plymouth)
- ¾ ounce sweet vermouth
- ¾ ounce green chartreuse
- 1 dash orange bitters

1. In a mixing glass, combine all ingredients with ice and stir.

2. Strain into a chilled coupe glass and garnish with a cocktail cherry or lemon peel.

··· SHERRY COBBLER ···

In the 1830s, this was *the* thing to sip on a hot day at Niblo's Garden in SoHo. The bar, an actual garden, was in a building's lush (in more ways than one) backyard at a time when there was considerably more space downtown. An entire Bohemian theater movement grew from the summer gatherings at this bar. Bartender William Niblo owned the bar, and his wife, Martha King Niblo, made most of the drinks.

GARNISH: seasonal berries, mint and a straw
GLASSWARE: Collins or julep cup

- 3.5 ounces Amontillado or dry Oloroso sherry
- 1 tablespoon sugar
- 2–3 orange slices

1. Muddle the orange and sugar in the bottom of a shaker. Add sherry and ice, then shake.

2. Strain into a tall glass or julep cup filled with crushed ice. Garnish and sip through a straw.

This little number is Harry Johnson's precursor to the Martini. His recipe called for anisette, but in the 1904 reprint of *Stuart's Fancy Drinks and How To Mix Them*, Thomas Stuart nixes that ingredient. In many ways, anisette is is the Marmite of the drinks world—you love it or you hate it.

GARNISH: orange peel or cherry
(Johnson's version calls for the latter)
GLASS: coupe

• 2 ouncea gin
• 1 ounce dry vermouth

• 2 dashes orange bitters

Stir all ingredients in a mixing glass with ice. Strain into a chilled coupe. Garnish.

A History — of the Highball in New York

Spirits brand consultant Robin Robinson has shared the following tidbit, as told to him by historian David Wondrich: Around the 1890s, a bartender named Patrick Duffy worked at an establishment on 22nd St and 4th Ave (now Park Ave South) which, like most bars, served Scotch whiskey straight from a cask—always a blend, and usually hot and mixed with spices. There he was often visited by a visiting British actor who would inquire about specific blends—"Mr. Dewars or Mr. Usher?" During that time, the actor asked for his Scotch in a curious way: over ice and diluted with phosphate or soda water. This became a popular drink in that time, leading to several innovations.

One noteworthy innovation was made in upstate New York, where they served different iterations at lake resorts. A local songstress would regularly order what we now call sangria, until one day the bar ran out of wine. The bartender replaced it with Scotch whiskey, she suggested adding lime and sugar and it caught on with her name attached: Mamie Taylor. Over time, the juices were narrowed down to just lime, soda water and ginger. Thus, a drink was born.

GOING GATSBY

" 'HE'S A BOOTLEGGER,' SAID THE YOUNG LADIES, MOVING
SOMEWHERE BETWEEN HIS COCKTAILS AND HIS
FLOWERS . . .'REACH ME A ROSE, HONEY, AND POUR ME A LAST
DROP INTO THAT CRYSTAL GLASS.' "

—excerpt from The Great Gatsby by F. Scott Fitzgerald

No other popular work quite evokes the not-so-secret lives of the 1920s drinking classes as well as *Gatsby*. Much of it was written in New York City, and many passages feature the city as a character unto itself. Nearly a century later we're still nostalgic for those Jazz Age lawn parties. So in the spirit of the characters in East Egg, here are five Prohibition–era cocktails to try. Note that these recipes all call for fresh juices—a key ingredient during the era, as most of the hooch was pretty rough stuff.

··· BEES KNEES ···

The name for this cocktail is both a reference to its honey ingredient and a play on a popular slang term of the era that means "the best." As in, I think you are simply the bees knees, dahling.

GARNISH: lemon twist

GLASS: coupe

- 2 ounces dry gin
- ¾ ounce lemon juice
- ¾ ounce honey syrup

Shake the ingredients with ice. Strain into a chilled coupe and garnish. Hold demurely and exclaim, "I'd like to just get one of those pink clouds and put you in it and push you around."

This drink is named for the Canadian-American silent movie star, and was created in Cuba, where many people fled to drink during Prohibition. According to Anistatia Miller and Jared Brown in *Cuban Cocktails*, the original recipe is attributed to barman Fred Kaufman of at the Hotel Nacional de Cuba. This version has been tweaked, but only a little.

GARNISH: This drink has enough flavor
without the garnish, but some extra cherry won't hurt!
GLASS: coupe or Martini

- ½ ounce white rum (use Havana Club real Cuban rum if you can find it. If not, use a good Caribbean white rum such as Banks 5 Island.)
- 1½ ounces pineapple juice
- 1 teaspoon grenadine
- 6 drops maraschino liqueur (such as Luxardo)

Add all the ingredients to a cocktail shaker and fill with ice. Shake, and strain into a chilled cocktail glass.

··· SIDECAR ···

There are so many variations on this orangey drink. I prefer this classic version with Cognac and enough lemon juice to keep it from being cloyingly sweet.

GARNISH: lemon twist

GLASS: coupe with optional sugar rim

- 1½ ounce Cognac
- ¾ ounce Cointreau
- ¾ ounce lemon juice

Rim the coupe glass with sugar if desired. Shake all ingredients with ice, strain into the glass and garnish.

··· CORPSE REVIVER № 2 ···

This drink appears in Harry Craddock's *Savoy Cocktail Book*, but the only reason the German-born bartender was even at the London hotel was because he was forced to move from New York. This is one of his more famous drinks—a brunch cocktail before there really was such a thing—and it aims to wake the spirit after a long night of partying. The original recipe calls for Kina Lillet, which no longer exists—but Cocchi Americano is a pretty close facsimile. My parents and I have a tradition of ordering this drink while out on the town on Easter Sunday.

GARNISH: lemon twist

GLASSWARE: coupe

- ¾ ounce dry gin
- ¾ ounce lemon juice
- ¾ ounce Cointreau
- ¾ ounce Cocchi Aperitivo Americano
- small barspoon or light mist of absinthe

1. Add all ingredients to a shaker with ice and shake. If you're misting the absinthe, don't add it to the shaker. Just mist once the mixture is in the glass.

2. Strain into a coupe glass and garnish.

It's not a real party until someone pops open the bubbly! This is such an elegant cocktail, especially considering it's named after a rifle used by the French in World War I.

GARNISH: lemon twist

GLASS: flute or coupe

- 1½ ounce gin
- ½ ounce fresh lemon juice
- ½ simple syrup
- sparkling wine (preferably Champagne)

1. Shake first three ingredients with ice. Strain into glass.

2. Top with bubbly and garnish.

Speakeasies

As modern drinkers fell in love with the classics all over again, nostalgia for Prohibition speakeasies grew just as fast. It's become fashionable again to open a bar with unmarked entrances, secret doorways or a required set of passwords. Al Hirschfeld's *The Speakeasies of 1932* is an excellent resource for learning more about the real thing; the celebrated caricaturist spotlights some of his favorite illegal spots in the city, noting their best drinks and his favorite bartenders. It's a blast to read about them and figure out which buildings stand in their place today. Still, in this age of legal drinking, jumping through hoops to get a good drink may seem more irritating than romantic. But at least the law won't show up and start shooting bottles off the wall, right? These venues have kept the speakeasy vibe alive—and are worth a few inconveniences.

'21' Club
21 West 52nd Street
New York, NY 10019
(212) 582-7200
21club.com

It makes sense to begin with one of the city's original and most enduring speakeasies. Here "club" is a relative term, as there is no membership per se. Almost anyone can enter '21' as long as they know how to clean up well (men are still required to wear jackets and ties and denim is frowned upon). It opened as a speakeasy by cousins Jack Kriendler and Charlie Berns on New Year's Eve 1929, with a hidden wine cellar that is still in use. Behind the bar, which has since been moved across the room, automatically-collapsing shelves would discard its bottles down a series of chutes into the sewer system below—a complicated system to protect from the snooping feds. In the 1980s, when construction began on the Paley Center next door, it was said the scent of alcohol still emanated from the foundation.

The former Bar Room is now its main dining room, with red checker–clothed tables that have sat dozens of celebrity regulars, like Frank Sinatra, the Marx Brothers, Humphrey Bogart, Dorothy Parker, Yankees owner George Steinbrenner, Bette Midler, members of British royalty and several sitting and former presidents. Even to this day, the likes of Alec Baldwin, Ricky Gervais, Bill Murray and Whoopie Goldberg still make a point of passing through that famous Iron Gate. Ernest Hemingway would drink his Papa Dobles here, though on an off night he would his regular order: "Since I'm not drinking, I'll just have a tequila."

Crowds of *tchotchkes* (New York-ese for "knickknacks") and artifacts of bygone decades adorn the Bar Room's walls and ceiling, along with a collection of cartoons from famous illustrators—most notably Walt Disney, Elize Segar, Peter Arno, Bill Gallo and Gene Ahern. During the Depression, artistic regulars paid their tab by contributing paintings that still hang in the foyer, lounge and Remington Room. It's practically a museum to artist Frederic Remington, housing 25 of his paintings.

While '21' boasts one of the most extensive wine lists in the city, it is also a fine place for a cocktail. A Martini is the iconic choice, but through the years, its signature drink has been the Southside—a tall, refreshing concoction that's a bit like a gin Julep. Born here before travelling the world over, it's a riff on the Major Bailey, which was the house drink at Jack and Charlie's former bar, the Puncheon on West 49th Street.

··· THE SOUTHSIDE ···

GARNISH: fresh mint

GLASS: Collins

- 2 ounce gin (bar uses Tanqueray)
- 1 ounce mint simple syrup (add several sprigs of mint while preparing the standard 1:1 recipe and strain)
- 4–5 fresh mint leaves
- juice of one lemon
- splash of soda

1. Vigorously shake all ingredients with ice in order to work that mint.

2. Strain into a Collins glass and garnish with fresh mint.

PDT

113 St. Mark's Place
New York, NY 10009
(212) 614-0386
pdtnyc.com

One of worst kept secrets in the city is PDT, which ironically stands for Please Don't Tell. One enters by using the 1940s payphone stall in Crif Dogs next door—press the button and wait to be monitored and buzzed in. It opened in 2007 with an impressive list by Jim Meehan, fresh off his job helming the cocktail program at Gramercy Tavern. For a bar that was supposed to be on the down low, it never was—instantly drawing publicity and accolades, including the number one spot on the World's 50 Best Bars list in 2011. Meehan is busy consulting in other cities these days, but the bar still draws top talent under the direction of Jeff Bell.

RAINES LAW ROOM AND DEAR IRVING

48 West 17th St.
New York, NY 10011
raineslawroom.com
55 Irving Place
New York, NY 10003
no phone
dearirving.com

Here's the recipe for Whiskey Business, one of the most popular drinks at Dear Irving and a fan favorite at the Bennett.

GARNISH: lemon wheel and ancho chili powder
GLASS: rocks/Old Fashioned

- 1 ounce Rittenhouse rye
- 1 ounce Ancho Reyes
- ½ ounce lemon juice
- ½ ounce cinnamon syrup (recipe below)

1. Shake with ice and strain into a glass over a large ice cube.

2. Garnish with lemon wheel sprinkled with ancho chile powder

Cinnamon Syrup

- 2 cups sugar
- 1 cup warm water
- 7 cinnamon sticks

Heat ingredients over low heat. Stir to dissolve sugar. Let sit overnight and strain cinnamon sticks out.

— *Spotlight: Meaghan Dorman* —

All of us wish we had a magic bell that could summon a cocktail whenever the craving struck. At Raines Law Room, Dear Irving and the Bennett that's precisely how one orders a drink. Meaghan Dorman began as the head bartender at Raines (named for a 19th-century law intended to curb drinking) in 2010 before going on to helm Dear Irving and the Bennett. Now with two locations (the second in the William Hotel near the Empire State Building), Raines Law room is an elegant Prohibition-era parlor with private, Orient Express-type seating arrangements. Dear Irving is like a dream apartment with, as Dorman describes it, "a *Midnight in Paris*" passage through decades of glamour. Of the three, the Bennett is the only street-level bar with signage, but it still shares that similar aesthetic. All three of these stylish speakeasy-style dens have an atmosphere committed to offering consistently good quality and ambience no matter the night of the week.

"Raines opened during the last call on speakeasies before people started to slag them," says Dorman. It set itself apart by making guests feel as though they were in someone's home; the bar in the back is even referred to as the "kitchen." Dear Irving feels more like a proper bar, and its menu goes in a more whimsical direction, "taking more liberties with the classics." By the time the Bennett opened in Tribeca, customers of both bars had favorite house cocktails, so the bar offered an "audience awards" menu to attract regulars.

Dorman is the co-founder of the charity LUPEC (Ladies United for the Preservation of Cocktails) and a frequent Speed Rack (see page 318) judge. Having mentored many careers, she's the ultimate bar mom. While passing on her mature approach, she says, "Bars are the last sacred adult space." Amen to that.

Angel's Share

8 Stuyvesant Street
New York, NY 1003
(212) 777-5415

Opened in 1994, Angel's Share was one of the first bars on the fore-front of the burgeoning modern cocktail scene. The entrance to the Japanese cocktail bar is notoriously hard to find (one enters through the Village Yokocho restaurant, but it's still not very obvious where to go from there), yet long lines still form almost every night. Its draw lies in its dedication to impeccable service, not to mention spectacu-lar, creative cocktails from a talented staff that are served in a dreamy setting. One of its earliest regulars was none other than Sasha Pe-traske, who used the experience as inspiration for Milk & Honey (see page 247). As of this writing, there is also a hidden sister bar down the street above Sharaku restaurant, open only Thursday–Saturday.

··· FLIRTBIRD ···

Created by bartender Takuma Watanabe, this take on the Jungle Bird makes artful use of Japanese ingredients.

GARNISH: shiso leaf

GLASS: Japanese clay tea cup or rocks/Old Fashioned glass

- 1½ ounces Mizu 'Saga Barley' Shochu
- 1 ounce yuzu juice
- ½ ounce agave syrup
- 2 shiso leaves (1 for garnish)
- Taiwanese plum powder (for rim)

1. Rim the cup with the plum powder.

2. Tear shiso leaf and add to shaker with the rest of the contents. Shake with ice and strain into the cup with 1 large cube of ice.

3. Garnish with 1 whole shiso leaf.

FLASK DRINKS

One of the lasting images from the Prohibition era is that of the iconic flapper girl, cheekily raising her skirt to display a flask held by a garter belt. Unsurprisingly, one of the enduring regulations since Repeal is the open container law. Though it is not often enforced, one might pay a hefty fine if caught drinking alcohol in the street—especially if they're using an obvious vessel like a glass or bottle.

There is, however, no law against swigging hooch from a flask.

Both of these cocktails are served at their respected establishments from a flask. Here's how to make your own:

This recipe was created by Chris Elford, now owner of No Anchor and Navy Strength in Seattle.

◆❖◆

GARNISH: orange twist

GLASS: 100-ml flask or coupe

- ¾ ounce Meletti amaro
- ¾ ounce Bonal gentian
- ¾ ounce London dry gin (bar uses Beefeater)
- ¾ ounce rye whiskey (bar uses Rittenhouse)
- 2 dashes Bittermens tiki bitters

Stir all ingredients with plenty of ice to chill and dilute. Serve up, or in a 100-ml flask with an orange twist expressed over the top and dropped in the drink.

··· LOUISIANA PURCHASE PUNCH ···

Head bartender Nick Bennett mixes up a large batch of this punch to be served in flasks at Porchlight Bar. This large-format recipe offers the choice between dropping all the ingredients in a bowl and serving as a magnificent punch, or dividing the liquid into individual 100-ml flasks. In other words, it's perfect for a Prohibition party!

- 1000 ml Domain de Canton ginger liqueur
- 750 ml bourbon (bar uses Medley Bros.)
- 750 ml Amontillado sherry
- 1000 ml brewed black tea
- 1000 ml Blenheim ginger beer
- 4 cups lemon juice
- 2½ cups oleo saccharum (recipe follows)

Add all ingredients to a large vessel and stir to combine. If serving from a punch bowl, add ice and stir until chilled. If serving from flasks, strain into individual flasks and refrigerate or keep on ice until cold.

Recipe for oleo saccharum

- peels of 8 lemons
- peels of 2 oranges
- 2½ cups granulated sugar

1. In a bowl, toss the peels with the sugar. Using some serious elbow grease, use a muddler or the back of a heavy wooden spoon to pound the peels until they express their oils.

2. Let sit for half an hour to an hour. Strain the liquid and discard the peels.

PORCHLIGHT

SUBWAY DRINKING TOUR

New York City is packed with fabulous watering holes. However, some neighborhoods lucked out with a higher concentration of quality cocktail bars that are within a few steps from one another, such as the connected Brooklyn neighborhoods of Carroll Gardens, Cobble Hill and Boerum Hill, a.k.a. the 'Barmuda Triangle.' Here is a recommended drinking tour that can be accessed by a single subway ride (well, unless the MTA has other plans, so always check mta.info for the latest transit update). So let's put on some walking (and drinking) shoes and head out on cocktail safari! Note: the natives are friendly and it's okay to feed us, but please do not point and aim flash cameras directly at us in our habitat. Also, it's a good idea to time your trip accordingly so as to be able to access your first bar and not to miss the last one. Be sure to drink plenty of water and order snacks!

Carroll Gardens/ Cobble Hill/Boerum Hill— a.k.a. "The Barmuda Triangle"

Train: F to Bergen Street

Bars: Clover Club, Leyenda, Grand Army, Le Boudoir, The Long Island Bar

First bar opens: 4 P.M. weekdays, noon weekends

Last bar closes: 2 A.M. weekends, midnight weekdays

Before the late 1990s, this South Brooklyn neighborhood was mostly residential, with few options for dining out—let alone drinking. By the early 2000s, it had exploded into a new gourmet frontier. Cocktails were slow to arrive, but when they did, they arrived quickly. Starting with Clover Club, it seemed that a new fine drinking establishment opened every week, each with its own unique personality and clientele.

It makes sense to begin this journey with the pioneer. Once you exit the F train at the front end, on the Warren Street exit, walk just a couple of blocks ahead on Smith Street to Clover Club.

I Clover Club
210 Smith Street
Brooklyn, NY 11201
(718) 855-7939
cloverclubny.com

It's impossible to fathom now, but when Clover Club opened on Smith Street in 2008, it was hard to find a good cocktail in Brooklyn. Julie Reiner, who had successfully run Manhattan's Flatiron Lounge, wanted to open a place near her family in Park Slope. As she was deciding on its location, drinks writer David Wondrich (see page 58) persuaded her to fill a void in Carroll Gardens—not entirely selflessly, as he lives within stumbling distance. Differentiating itself from Park Slope, the neighborhood is less family-oriented, housing many writers, artists and publishers. Or as Reiner puts it, the space had "people who would frequent a cocktail bar within walking distance."

Though not a speakeasy, the decor has a simple 1920s elegance to it—it's quite spacious, with fine wood paneling, tiled floors, patterned tin ceilings and chandeliers. There is a romantic parlor room in the back that has its own bar, loveseats and a fireplace. The main bar area is railed off to allow servers and customers to pass across the room freely. Reiner noticed a difference in the clientele right away. "In Manhattan, if people weren't spilling drinks on each other, it wasn't fun. People in Brooklyn wanted to sit. And eat." Though delicious, the food was mostly small plates pub fare for a while, but Reiner quickly learned this gourmet crowd wanted full meals. Adjustments were made immediately.

Of course, Clover Club's main attraction is its drink menu. Aside from the namesake Clover Club Prohibition-era cocktail, the drinks selection rotates seasonally, offering classics, variations, royales, sours, hot drinks and large-format punches. Most of the beverages are originals created by Reiner and her talented protégés, including Katie Stipe, Franky Marshall, Giuseppe González, Tom Macy, Ivy Mix (with whom Reiner partnered to open Leyenda across the street), Brad Farran, Nathan Dumas and Lacy Hawkins.

··· GREEN GIANT ···

Feeling springy? This sugar snap-pea drink from Tom Macy is a surefire sign that spring has sprung in Brooklyn.

◆◆◆

GARNISH: 1 sugar snap pea
GLASS: rocks/Old Fashioned

- 4 sugar snap peas, trimmed and snapped in half
- 8 to 10 fresh tarragon leaves
- ¾ ounce simple syrup
- 2 ounces Old Tom gin (bar uses Hayman's)
- ½ ounce dry vermouth
- ¾ ounce lemon juice
- crushed ice

1. In the bottom of a shaker, muddle the snap peas and tarragon with the simple syrup.

2. Add the other ingredients and shake with ice cubes. Double-strain into a rocks glass over crushed ice.

3. Top by inserting the sugar snap pea into the ice. Making sure top is removed.

II LEYENDA

221 Smith St
Brooklyn, NY 11201
(347) 987-3260
leyendabk.com

Almost directly across Smith Street from Clover Club is Leyenda, opened in 2015 by Reiner, her partner Susan Fedroff and bartender Ivy Mix. The bar is overseen by Mix, (yes, that's really her given last name—it was destined to be), who wanted to bring this part of Brooklyn some much-needed Latin culture. She does so through her exquisite cocktails, from highballs to margaritas to breezy agave-based fantasies. The spirits on the back bar are displayed in various decorative "spirit boxes," like deities. The scrumptious food menu under executive chef Sue Torres is a Central and South American tour of snacks and mostly small plates (tacos, pupusas, arepas, etc.), in addition to a couple of larger entrées and an outstanding brunch (with homemade sangritas and horchata you can get with any spirit). It's been said that Leyenda is so warm and convivial that it's almost a religious experience to spend time there. So it makes sense that the back of the restaurant has old church pews for seats.

Considered the house drink at Leyenda, Ivy Mix's tropical nod to her business partner Julie Reiner (who is from Hawaii) makes excellent use of its Leyendified splashes of mezcal and rum.

GARNISH: mint sprig, lime wheel
and orchid (if available)
GLASS: rocks

- 1 ounce Del Maguey Vida mezcal
- 1 ounce Appleton Signature rum
- ¾ ounce lime juice
- ½ ounce toasted almond orgeat
- ½ ounce Pierre Ferrand Dry Curaçao

Shake all ingredients with ice and strain into a rocks glass over crushed ice. Garnish.

Hopefully you've had a little nosh, because there are at least two more stops to make! Head out the door, turn right, heading north on Smith Street past Baltic and continue walking till you cross Atlantic Avenue. Hang a right and walk to State Street, then head left for one block.

III GRAND ARMY

336 State Street
Brooklyn, NY 11217
(718) 422-7867
grandarmybar.com

Grand Army is usually packed, but it's worth it to find a corner. Co-owner Damon Boelte left Prime Meats on the south end of the neighborhood to serve as head tender at this homey venue, which also includes a stellar beer program by Chris Balla (and decent wine, too). Toward the back is a massive raw bar—bivalves are served with some dozen or so different sauces in nifty test tube droppers. But the seasonal cocktail menu is the star of the show, and isn't that why you schlepped to Brooklyn?

> If you still have it in you, walk back to Atlantic Avenue. The next stop is a few blocks up, about 15 minutes. Or you can fairly easily hop in a cab or call/use an app for a car service. If you prefer to walk things off a bit, stroll up Atlantic to Clinton St. Look for the restaurant Chez Moi on the right. Your next destination is accessible through its door.

IV Le Boudoir

135 Atlantic Avenue
Brooklyn, NY 11201
(347) 227-8337
boudoirbk.com
opens at 6

The press promotes this underground bar as one modeled after Marie Antoinette's bedroom, but head bartender Franky Marshall (a Clover Club alum) maintains that it is just meant to evoke a French renaissance–style elegance, so one feels as though they've stepped into a luxurious parlor (complete with piano). The bar area only holds a few seats, but loveseat vignettes are spaced throughout. More exciting is that the semi-private back room and privy (one of the coolest in the whole city—let them pull chain flushes!) are in what used to be an Atlantic Avenue subway tunnel, closed since the early 20th century. The cocktails are fabulous—combining well curated spirits and imaginative, bold flavors. Small bites from the restaurant upstairs are also available.

Franky Marshall has quite the way with outside-the-box (and in-the-spice-rack) ingredients. This spicy-chocolaty cocktail is a perfect example of her flavor mastery.

GARNISH: sprinkle of cacao nibs and a star anise
GLASS: coupe in a bowl just big enough to hold it with ice

- 2 dashes Chocolate Chili Bitters
- ½ ounce demerara syrup
- ½ ounce chile liqueur (such as Ancho Reyes)
- 1 ounce absinthe
- 1¼ ounces toasted coconut almond milk

1. Place glass in bowl and build all ingredients in the glass.

2. Add pebble ice to the bowl, then into the cocktail. Stir.

3. Garnish with cacao nibs and star anise.

··· SORCIÈRE ···

This is another magical concoction from sorceress Franky Marshall.

GARNISH: see below (ruins the joke otherwise)
GLASS: chalice or coupe

- ¼ ounce cinnamon bark syrup (make 1:1 simple syrup with several cinnamon sticks, cool and strain)
- ½ ounce fresh lemon juice
- ½ ounce aquavit
- ¾ ounce blanco tequila
- 1 ounce Mastiha Liqueur

1. Add all ingredients to a mixing tin. Shake with ice.

2. Finely strain into the chalice. Garnish with twine-bound twigs from a witch's broom.

> You came this far. Ready for a nightcap? It's just across the street. Walk to the corner of Henry. Look for the neon— you can't miss it.

V THE LONG ISLAND BAR

110 Atlantic Avenue
Brooklyn, NY 11201
(718) 625-8908
thelongislandbar.com
(see page 256 for full profile)

End your tour at this fine neighborhood saloon, a revamped classic diner, with one of Toby Cecchini's incredible gimlets or a Boulevardier. Perhaps you're hungry for one of the greatest burgers in the city, or maybe some buffalo fried cauliflower. Go on, you've earned it. Take a picture with the NO DANCING sign. From here you can easily catch a cab back to where you are staying.

THE VISIONARIES (AND

THEIR SIGNATURE DRINKS)

There is a profound pleasure in sipping a perfectly balanced Martini or Manhattan, or a Corpse Reviver with just the right hint of absinthe. Any bartender who strives to create a classic cocktail with such precision of flavor and presentation is already doing the lord's work. But throughout the city there are bartenders whose creative vision outpaces any expectation. Here's a look at some of the mavericks of the New York bar culture and their finest creations.

"SOMETHING'S ALWAYS
HAPPENING HERE. IF YOU'RE
BORED IN NEW YORK, IT'S YOUR
OWN FAULT."
—*Myrna Loy*

DEATH & CO

433 East 6th Street
New York, NY 10009
(212) 388-0882
deathandcompany.com

Opened on New Year's Eve of 2006, Death & Co is considered one of the most influential bars in the city. The names of those who have worked behind the stick tell quite the story on their own—Phil Ward, Brian Miller, Alex Day (who became co-owner, along with David Kaplan and Ravi DeRossi), Joaquín Simó, Eryn Reece, Thomas Waugh, Don Lee, Brad Farran, Jessica Gonzalez, Scott Teague, Jason Littrell, Jillian Vose, each a tremendous mixologist in their own right. Some call the staff here the Yankees of bartending; I'm a Mets fan, but even I can see the connection between baseball's premiere franchise and the dream team at Death & Co. They've created some of the most influential cocktails of the last decade or so: Oaxacan Old Fashioned, Flor de Jerez, Naked and Famous, The Conference, Orange Julius and more. And after all this time, it's still a terrific place for a drink if you can get

in. If you can't get in, it's worth asking the doorman for advice on when to return.

Any discussion of New York's drinks scene must include this East Village pioneer, whose talented team produced several recipes that bars across the globe now use.

T his was a smoky apple brandy Old Fashioned originally created at Dram, but it was refined for Death & Co, where it landed on the menu around 2011." —*Jason Littrell,* creator

GARNISH: none

GLASS: rocks/Old Fashioned

- **Two dashes Angostura Bitters**
- **1 demerara syrup (2:1)**
- **¼ ounce peated Scotch whiskey**
- **¾ ounce bourbon**
- **1½ ounces Laird's Bonded Apple Brandy**

Stir all ingredients with ice until well chilled. Strain into the glass over a large ice cube.

Here's a crowd favorite created by Phil Ward that is still in popular demand.

GARNISH: 1 lemon twist

GLASS: coupe

- 2 ounces Beefeater gin
- 1 ounce Dolin dry vermouth
- ½ ounce Cointreau
- 3 dashes Vieux Pontarlier absinthe

Stir all the ingredients over ice, then strain into a coupe. Garnish with the lemon twist.

T his cocktail [created at Death & Co] is the bastard child born out of an illicit Oaxacan love affair between the classic Last Word and the Paper Plane, a drink Sam Ross created at the West Village bar Little Branch. Choosing an aggressively smoky, funky mezcal was key here, as there is relatively little of it in the drink and it needs to stand up against two liqueurs, neither of which lacks complexity." —*Joaquín Simó*

GARNISH: none

GLASS: coupe

- ¾ ounce Del Maguey Chichicapa mezcal
- ¾ ounce Yellow Chartreuse
- ¾ ounce Aperol
- ¾ ounce lime juice

Shake all the ingredients with ice, then strain into a coupe.

DRAM

177 South 4th Street
Brooklyn, NY 11211
(718) 486-3726
drambar.com

··· BEHIND GOD'S BACK ···

This yummy drink comes from Jason Littrell's tenure at Dram, circa 2010.

GARNISH: mint sprig

GLASS: hurricane or pilsner

- ¼ ounce sugar cane syrup
- ¼ ounce cinnamon syrup
- ¼ ounce orgeat
- ½ ounce pineapple juice
- ¾ ounce lime juice
- 2 ounces Chairman's Reserve Rum
- 2 dashes each Peychaud's and Angostura bitters

1. Combine ingredients in a pilsner or hurricane glass with crushed ice, and swizzle.

2. Top with fresh ice, float both bitters on top and finish off with more fresh ice. Garnish with a lavish sprig of mint.

A very simple riff on a Negroni: smoky mezcal replaces the usual piney gin, a gentian- and quinine-bittered apertif (Bonal) subs for the traditional wormwood-bittered, fortified wine (sweet vermouth), and an artichoke-driven amaro takes the place of the classic Campari. There's a chemical found in artichokes that makes the flavor of chocolate more pronounced on our palate, hence the addition of the chocolate, chile and nut flavored Mole bitters." —*Joaquín Simó*

GARNISH: none

GLASS: Nick & Nora (or coupe)

- 1 ounce Vida Mezcal
- 1 ounce Bonal
- 1 ounce Cynar

- 1 dash Bittermens Mole bitters.

Combine all ingredients in a mixing glass, add ice and stir briskly. Strain into a chilled Nick & Nora glass. No garnish.

I just wanted to be able to walk into a bar and get a good says Joaquín Simó, owner of Pouring Ribbons in the East When he started out as a bartender in New York City, it wa to get a job as a bartender unless you'd already *been* a ba here. He worked his way up the system with a succession rant bar gigs for a couple of years before he could apply t bar. "Milk & Honey, Pegu Club, Little Branch—these were lands in the sea." Restaurants were just beginning to add program to their menus, and only a handful used fresh ing and quality spirits. For instance, Simó had been working i the-radar South American restaurant that offered six diffe four of which were single-variety.

Before the smartphone era, he went around town with per—a running list of where the top bartenders (Sammy Maloney, Micky McIlroy, Jim Kearns, etc.) were working a nights they worked. "Follow the bartender" was something many up-and-coming bartenders did back then to network. When he learned a David Kaplan and Ravi DeRossi were opening a new bar in the East Village, Simó landed himself a gig at Death & Co.

The speakeasy style of bars—seen at places like Milk & Honey and PDT—had "struck a nerve" with New York City drinkers. Sasha Petraske famously shunned publicity at Milk & Honey, going so far as to change the number if he felt too many people knew about it (to drink at M&H required calling a number and knowing a password). Conversely, Death & Co found themselves in the *New York Times* Sunday Style section within their first month.

Taking a page from London's cocktail playbook, they soon set themselves apart from the New York scene by offering an extensive menu of 60 to 80 original drinks and paying more attention to little details like ice. As another innovation, the bartenders themselves began to run the bar, beginning with Phil Ward. "The inmates were running the asylum," says Simó with a chuckle.

When Ward left Death & Co to open Mayahuel down the street in 2009, he began a new era in NYC cocktail culture: bars *owned* by bartenders. In 2012, Simó opened Pouring Ribbons. After working with Death & Co for five and a half years, he says one of the biggest challenges for bar owners these days is keeping staff interested and motivated to stay, rather than lured away by gigs at new establishments. Bartenders are no longer required to have NYC experience in order to get a job; high-end cocktail programs exist in so many places all over the world and it's easy enough to check references. "I know where to send people in cities I've never even been to," Simó says. Still, "I am excited if I can keep someone a year to two years tops."

It may be hard to keep a loyal bartender on staff these days, but the silver lining for us is that it's much easier to find a good Daiquiri almost anywhere— or at least establishments that "speak Negroni or speak Martini." As Simó says, "The enduring legacies of bars like Death & Co are not all about the shirt garters or the facial hair . . .when I order a drink at a neighborhood restaurant and the vermouth is kept in the fridge, I think, 'we won!'"

THE WOOLY

11 Barclay Street
New York, NY 10007
(646) 807-9665
thewooly.com

Eryn Reece, another talented Death & Co alum, is now the beverage director of the re-vamped Wooly, tucked inside the Woolworth building downtown. Who doesn't love a bal-anced tropical drink served in an elephant tiki mug?

The house tiki drink at the Wooly manages to be fruity without being overly sweet. It's a great excuse to pick up some of that delicious peach liqueur too.

GARNISH: fresh mint sprig

GLASS: tiki mug (preferably elephant-shaped)

- 1½ ounces Greenhook Ginsmiths Old Tom gin
- ¾ ounce Ancho Verde chili liqueur
- 1 ounce lime juice
- ½ ounce Aperol
- ½ ounce passionfruit juice
- 1 teaspoon Ginger
- 1 teaspoon Cinnamon
- 1 teaspoon Giffard Peche liqueur

1. Dry shake all ingredients for 10 to 15 seconds.

2. Shake with ice for 15 more seconds. Strain into tiki mug over ice pellets or crushed ice and garnish.

We're in the post–punk rock era now," says bartender Frank Cisneros. And indeed, modern cocktail history does follow a similar timeline to independent rock music: the Dale DeGroff era was ska, and "2007 was the year the cocktail broke." Cisneros is referring to the impact felt by innovators such as Pegu Club, PDT and Death & Co, which were celebrating early anniversaries when Dram, a Williamsburg bar owned by Tom Chadwick, first opened. It happens constantly now, but back then introducing a cocktail bar to Williamsburg was still a punk thing to do. It was here that Cisneros, who had been practicing cocktail recipes with Chadwick at dives like Bushwick Country Club, became a full-time cocktail bartender.

From there, Cisneros honed those skills at Prime Meats (alongside Damon Boelte, who now owns Grand Army; see page 104) in Carroll

Gardens and the Drink in Williamsburg. Then a surprising thing happened. In 2014, Cisneros was given a job opportunity to train bartenders at the Mandarin Oriental Hotel in Tokyo, and he took it.

Japanese bartenders are quite distinguished in their own right, so why did they need a New Yorker to show them how it's done? "You have to remember there was no Prohibition in Japan. They've been doing everything the same way in western style bars since the 1880s . . .They've never had to rediscover techniques or ingredients. At western hotel bars like the Mandarin, because their presentation is so specific, they buy all their syrups. They're afraid of inconsistency." The task wasn't easy, and Cisneros had to overcome many humbling experiences. "It was the case of the teacher being the student."

Aspects of the cocktail culture differ from the American experience in several ways. For one thing, high-end cocktail bars tend to be very quiet, with no background music. There's little chitchat, especially among the bartenders. Even the ordinary bar sounds—stirring, placing ice into glasses, etc.—are done as quietly as possible. The practice of *omotenashi*, "selfless hospitality," is in full effect. For example, if a guest wants to know the best place to eat Yakitori, not only will the bar provide the address, they will send someone to escort that person to their destination. "[In Japan] it's an affordable luxury to be alone with your cocktail."

New Yorkers will soon experience for themselves what Cisneros learned from his year abroad. In the meantime, you can make one of his signature cocktails, the Margot Tenenbaum, named after a (very post-punk) character from Wes Anderson's *The Royal Tenenbaums*.

··· MARGOT TENENBAUM ···

GARNISH: none

GLASS: coupe

- 2 ounces bourbon (Buffalo Trace or another high-rye-content bourbon)
- ¾ ounce fresh lemon juice
- ½ ounce honey syrup
- ½ ounce Zucca Rabarbaro amaro

Shake all ingredients with ice. Strain into a coupe.

AMOR Y AMARGO

443 East 6th Street
New York, NY 10009
(212) 614- 6818
AmoryAmargoNY.com
No reservations accepted

"We're like a bumblebee— small, but mighty," says Amor y Amargo's beverage director, Sother Teague. "They're not aerodynamically sound and should not fly, but yet they do." And this bumblebee of a bar, whose name is Spanish for "love and bitter," was only ever intended to be a popup. Originally conceived by Avery and Janet Glasser of Bittermens Bitters and Ravi DeRossi (co-owner of Death & Co, Cienfuegos and Mother of Pearl), its goal was to open New Yorkers' minds to the world of bitter drinks. Along the way, the Glassers went out, Teague came in, and the tiny bar has endured as a neighborhood and industry favorite.

Says Sother Teague: "This is an oldie that's remained on the menu for long after its creator left us for greener pastures. It's a big drink with big flavors. Smoky from mezcal and savory from Kümmel, (caraway, cumin and fennel seed liqueur), it gets a strong backbone from rye. The apple bitters add a perfumy finish. Sip this one while listening to some rag-time tunes on an old Steinway."

GARNISH: none

GLASS: coupe

- 1 ½ ounces Rittenhouse rye
- ¾ ounce Carpano Antica Formula vermouth
- ½ ounce mezcal
- ¼ ounce Kümmel liqueur
- 2 dashes apple bitters

Stir all ingredients until chilled. Strain into coupe glass.

··· VALENTINE'S GRAPEFRUIT ···

This stirred cocktail from Lindsay Matteson plays a neat trick on the senses, tasting incredibly juicy despite not containing any juice!

GARNISH: grapefruit twist

GLASS: Collins glass

- ¾ ounce Carpano Bianco
- ¾ ounce Gran Classico
- ¾ ounce Fernet Branca
- 2 dashes Scrappy's Grapefruit Bitters

Add all ingredients in a Collins glass. Add ice and fill with club soda. Garnish with a grapefruit twist.

MOTHER OF PEARL

95 Avenue A
New York, NY 10009
(212) 614-6818
motherofpearlnyc.com
reservations encouraged

And now for something completely tiki! This former Gin Palace space has transformed into a tropical oasis, serving up Polynesian-inspired cocktails and substantial vegetarian bites. Under the direction of Jane Danger, the cocktails are well balanced (meaning not overly cloying) and feature spirits from practically every port of call. Their whimsical presentations go beyond the iconic totem mug—at least one person in your party has to order the Shark Eye. You're welcome.

CIENFUEGOS

95 Avenue A
New York, NY 10009
(212) 614-6818
cienfuegosny.com
reservations accepted

Cienfuegos, Spanish for "a hundred fires," is named for a Cuban port town that used to be a hub of rum trade. The stunning décor of this rum-centric venue indeed evokes tones of a breezy tropical escape. The cocktail list contains its own punch section in both large and small format, in addition to both tropical drinks and simpler stirred options. Like Mother of Pearl, the menu is entirely vegetarian, though the item has several options even a hungry carnivore can make peace with.

FORT DEFIANCE

365 Van Brunt Street
Brooklyn, NY 11231
(347) 453-6672
fortdefiancebrooklyn.com

With terrific comfort food and a meticulously curated cocktail program, this Hurricane Sandy survivor is one of the great prides of Red Hook. It also happens to serve one of the best Irish Coffees in town! This recipe come from owner St. John Frizell.

un fact: Laird's applejack was one of the first commercially marketed brandies in the US and has been around since 1780. This boozy, stirred drink makes fine use of it.

GARNISH: lemon twist

GLASS: coupe

- 1½ ounces Laird's Bonded Apple Brandy
- ¾ ounces Carpano Antica Formula
- ¾ ounce Cocchi Torino
- 1 dash Peychaud's bitters

Stir all ingredients with ice and strain into the cocktail glass. Garnish.

— Spotlight: Lucinda Sterling —

Grab the glass at the lowest point, not at the top, so as never to put fingers on a drink where lips go." This is one of many small but meaningful details passed on to Lucinda Sterling at Milk & Honey by her mentor, Sasha Petraske. She was one of the last people he trained, taking the reins at his bar Middle Branch before opening Seaborne, the venue in Red Hook, Brooklyn he was set to open before his untimely passing in 2015.

"Don't interrupt guests, don't interfere. Remove and replace napkins without them even noticing," was another service trick he taught Sterling, along with "Drop ice into a glass gently so it doesn't splash." These unexpected and meticulous levels of service make a noticeable difference—not to mention a super tidy atmosphere. It's not for every bartender, especially those who are used to high-volume nights and huge tips. Says Sterling, "A bartender who takes home only $150 a night really appreciates his or her craft."

Over the years Sterling has witnessed quite a few shifts in the way New Yorkers drink. It was once challenging to coax people away from Redbull and vodka, but now cocktail bar patrons are more typically part of the "educated drinking classes." They even know to request modern classics originally created at Milk & Honey, like the Old Maid or Medicina Latina. Sterling says, "The Madmen era introduced bourbon and people kept requesting drinks that were 'not too sweet' [In these instances, Petraske taught his staff to use honey syrup instead of simple.] Then it was spicy. Now they all want smoky."

"Fundamentally, what we're about is the classics that can be made with what's available," she says of the two bars. "Cocktails for a group shouldn't take more than one and a half minutes each to make and should arrive at the same time, " Petraske used to say. Why? So everyone can toast together.

Dutch Kills

27-24 Jackson Avenue
Long Island City, NY 11101
(718) 383-2724
dutchkillsbar.com

When Dutch Kills opened in 2010, Queens had yet to fully dive into the city's cocktail scene. By then, Manhattan and Brooklyn were deep into the post-Civil-War-era-meets-speakeasy style of drinkery. Sasha Petraske and Richard Boccato knew better than to open another paradigm of the Milk & Honey format in Long Island City; instead they went in a more cocktail-casual direction, drawing clientele not only from a thirsty, underserved neighborhood but as a destination bar for everyone else as well. On the next page is one of bartender Abraham Hawkins' most requested drinks.

GARNISH: orange twist

GLASS: rocks/Old Fashioned

- 1 dash of Angostura bitters
- 2 dashes chocolate bitters
- ⅜ ounce maple syrup
- 1 ounce Islay Scotch (smoky)
- 1 ounce bourbon

Build in the glass, and add rock ice. Stir 10 to 15 times, and garnish with a long orange twist.

FRESH KILLS

161 Grand Street
Brooklyn, NY 11249
(718) 599-7888
freshkillsbar.com

Expanding on the success of Dutch Kills, Richard Boccato opened Fresh Kills in Greenpoint, Brooklyn in 2016. Dragon's Breath is an adaptation of an R. De Fleury drink in *The Man Behind the Bar*, 1934.

··· DRAGON'S BREATH ···

GARNISH: lemon twist, pickled walnut (optional)
GLASS: coupe

- 5 drops (not dashes) of Tabasco
- 1 ounce apricot liqueur
- 1 ounce dry vermouth
- 1 ounce Calvados

1. Stir with ice and strain into a chilled coupe. Garnish with a lemon twist.

2. Serve with a pickled walnut on the side in a steel ramekin with two toothpicks.

──Spotlight: Robert Simonson──

For Robert Simonson, one of the most interesting things about the cocktail beat is discovering trends that are "new to us, but old as time." Bottled cocktails, rye, smoke, shrubs, even the wide variety of bitters—it's not that these things are new, it's that they had been forgotten and people are paying attention to them again. Even ice. "Ice? I never thought about ice before [writing about cocktails]. It's what got drinks cold."

Simonson began his writing career covering theater, but after a couple of decades he was ready to do something new. After taking classes at the International Wine and Spirit Trust, he entered the world of wine writing, but found it a bit stuffy. Luckily, he met Ann Rogers (before she was Ann Tuennerman, a.k.a. "Mrs. Cocktail" of the Tales of the Cocktail festival) who invited him to "this little cocktail thing" in New Orleans in 2006. This "opened the stage" to a world he didn't know existed—one filled with passionate mixologists, historians and fellow journalists.

He began writing about spirits and cocktails for the *New York Times* in 2009, but he's freelanced for other publications as well. He's the author of *The Old Fashioned: The Story of the World's Most Classic Cocktail* and *A Proper Drink: The Untold Story of How a Band of Bartenders Saved the Civilized Drinking World*. With so much of what we see in the cocktail arena being inventive re-imaginings of the classics, is there anything that's truly new? "OK. Draft cocktails. No one did that before."

Bar Pleiades

Surrey Hotel

20 East 76th Street
New York, NY 10021
(212) 772-2600
barpleiades.com

Bar Pleiades is a fabulous hotel bar is located just off the east-side offshoot of Café Boulud. This aromatic beauty comes courtesy of head bartender Darryl Chan.

··· PICTURING WILD FIELDS ···

GARNISH: lemon twist

GLASS: Nick & Nora

- 1 barspoon orgeat
- ¼ ounce Pür•likör Elderflower
- ½ ounce Suze liqueur
- ¾ ounce La Diablada Italia Pisco
- 1½ ounces Glenfiddich 12-Year Scotch

1. Combine all ingredients in mixing glass and stir with ice.

2. Strain into a chilled Nick & Nora glass. Garnish with lemon twist.

EMPLOYEES ONLY

510 Hudson Street
New York, NY 10014
(212) 242-3021
employeesonlynyc.com

The bartenders at Employees Only wear white double-breasted jackets as uniforms, and I admit that the first time I sat at the bar I wasn't sure if I should order a drink or provide a medical history intake. Originally opened in 2004 by a team of industry friends—Dushan Zaric, Henry LaFargue, Igor Hadzismajlovic, Jason Kosmas and Bill Gilroy—it has since opened outposts around the world, including Miami and Singapore, in addition to a sister bar in the city, Macao Trading Company. Turns out it's a lousy place to follow doctor's orders, unless those orders are to drink and eat creative, delicious things, like this romantic cocktail by Kosmas and Zaric.

GARNISH: crown of mint

GLASS: coupe

- 1½ ounces vodka
- 1 ounce puréed blackberries (recipe follows)
- ¾ ounce St-Germain Elderflower liqueur
- ½ ounce fresh lemon juice

1. Pour the vodka, liqueur, purée and juice in to a mixing glass. Add cold large ice cubes and shake vigorously.

2. Strain into a chilled cocktail glass. Place the crown of mint into your palm and smack it with your other hand to release the aroma. Gently place the mint on the surface of the cocktail and serve.

Blackberry Purée

- ¼ pound fresh or frozen, thawed blackberries (about 1 cup)
- 2 tablespoons superfine sugar
- 2 tablespoons water
- 2 tablespoons lemon juice, freshly squeezed

Combine all ingredients in a blender. Liquefy and strain through a coarse sieve. Recipe will keep for 3 to 4 days if refrigerated. Makes about 1 cup.

Spotlight: Eben Freeman

Eben Freeman decided to take the classic approach to bartending a few steps further, in some cases all the way into a science lab. He has carved a niche in the cocktail world working as the beverage director of restaurants like WD-50 and Tailor, where he worked with chefs like Wylie Dufresne and Sam Mason to invent cocktails that matched the cuisine. This involved employing what were then considered revolutionary techniques, such as fat-washing, smoking (his signature is a smoked cola) and molecular gastronomy (vodka and cranberry caviar, anyone?). In 2015, he opened Genuine Liquorette *(191 Grand Street, 646-726-4633)*, which maintains a respectful balance between serious cocktailing and playful modern mixing. He's a busy man these days, but was kind enough to impart some of his experience from the road.

ON EMBARKING ON THE CROSSROADS OF CUISINE AND COCKTAILS: "The first bartending job I had was in a Jamaican restaurant. The chef took pride in preparing all the house beverages we served at the bar—ginger beer, sorrel, sour sop and sea moss. From the start I took it for granted that the bar and kitchen work together and that the vocabulary must be shared. It was not some high-minded thing about culinary cocktails, it was just common sense that you served Jamaican drinks at a Jamaican restaurant."

ON WHETHER CHEFS GET WHAT BARTENDERS DO: "I could argue that many chefs do not get it and often have adversarial relationships with bartenders who receive more press, but that is another book perhaps. When William Grimes retired from reviewing restaurants, he said the thing that had the most impact on the restaurant world was the evolution of the bar. That evolution continues to this day, and guests now expect a top-notch restaurant to have not just solid classics but innovative serves, names and context that use local seasonal ingredients. A great steak is a great steak, but the beverage, be it wine or cocktails, has to transcend its category."

ON BARTENDER EXPECTATIONS IN RESTAURANTS IN NEW YORK AND BEYOND: "It used to be a rarity to find good drinks outside a major city; now you have great bars everywhere in the United States and beyond. The question is no longer, 'Is there a good bar where I am going?' It is, 'How many bars can I visit during my trip?' Remember that restaurants are in the business of selling. A more jaded view would be that things have only changed because bars started making money and a restaurant cannot survive with out those sales any more than a bar can survive in a major city without a kitchen increasing check averages."

RAINES LAW ROOM

48 West 17th St.
New York, NY 10011
At the William Hotel: 24 East 39th
Street
New York, 10016
no phone
raineslawroom.com

The first of these two sophisticated, parlor room–style cocktail lounges opened in 2010 at the apex of the speakeasy movement, with Meaghan Dorman as the head bartender. By the time the second location opened in 2014, the speakeasy–hidden bar format had opened up to allow for a relaxed yet equally elegant hotel lounge experience with a Victorian feel. The name is more ironic here, as the Raines Law of 1896 forbid the sale of alcohol on Sundays outside of hotels. In both locations, as the Morrissey song goes, every day is like Sunday, though neither silent nor gray.

This RLR beauty is an enduring classic, with flavors that play so well off of each other.

❖

GARNISH: brandied cherry

GLASS: coupe

- 2 dashes Bittermens Mole Bitters
- ½ ounce Del Maguey Crema de Mezcal
- 1 ounce cream sherry
- 1½ ounces Zacapa 23 rum

Stir with ice until chilled and strain into cocktail class. Garnish.

DEAR IRVING

(see bar info page 84)

While Raines Law Room is Meaghan Dorman's stage, Dear Irving is her baby, the first of the four bars she co-owns with the Raines team. Each room in this upstairs bar is styled thematically in separate eras; to walk through the venue, one steps from the late 1950s into 1930s glam into a back parlor decked out in French Renaissance toile splendor. The drinks will transport you as well—like this update on the French 75.

··· VICE VERSA ···

GARNISH: none

GLASS: large coupe

- ¾ ounce grapefruit juice
- ½ ounce Luxardo bitter
- ½ ounce Gifford Pamplemousse liqueur
- 1 ounce NY Distilling Dorothy Parker gin
- Rosé Cava (bar uses Raventos)

Shake all ingredients except Cava with ice. Strain into a large coupe. Top with cava.

THE BENNETT

134 West Broadway
New York, NY 10013
thebennettbar.com

The younger sibling of Dear Irving since 2016, The Bennett is first of the Raines-team bars with a sign and a street level entrance. The service bell ritual still holds in this Tribeca bar, but the bar is longer, the seating more open and the food menu more comprehensive. Here is one of Dorman's favorites:

GARNISH: apple slices

GLASS: zombie (tiki)

- **2 ounces granny smith and pear juice (recipe below)**
- **¾ ounce St-Germain liqueur**
- **1½ ounces La Diablada pisco**
- **orange blossom water**

1. For the granny smith and pear juice: Juice 2 granny smith apples for every one bartlett pear. Use tablespoon of Vitamin C powder to preserve color.

2. Shake ingredients hard with crushed ice and strain into glass. Top with more crushed ice.

3. Garnish with two apple slices and spritz of orange blossom water.

—Spotlight: Tom Richter—

With over 35 years of experience, Tom Richter has worked every position in a bar or restaurant except executive chef. He tended bars way back when every cocktail was shaken, during the sad sour mix days when there were " . . .a lot of weird shots." (Nuts and Berries, anyone?) There were no cocktail bars in New York. "Everyone's concentrated on having groovy whiskey now. Back then, you were lucky to have Scotch." There was no savoring what's in the glass—"people just drank to get hammered." The night clubs where he worked were "Speed Rack [see page 318] all night."

Many who approach the profession from this perspective don't go on to become cocktail bartenders. However, says Richter, "trying really delicious tastes is in line with what I like to do." In the mid-1980s, he worked at Zuni Café in San Francisco, his first bartending gig where he experienced drinks made with fresh juices, and he never looked back. It was just around this time that Dale DeGroff (see page 21) was reacquainting New Yorker drinkers with fresh produce at the Rainbow Room.

Like DeGroff, Richter is also an actor; he was even cast in what could have been a breakout role, *Silence: the Musical*, a Broadway play based on *Silence of the Lambs*. Sadly, the poster joins the others on Broadway restaurant Joe Allen's wall of flops. But Richter's star turn was about to come. While working at David Drake's in New Jersey, he developed his Tomr's Tonic syrup—with some added spritz, it was much better than the tonic coming out of most soda guns at the time and still elevates gin and tonics to this day.

After stints at the John Dory (under Sasha Petraske) and the Beagle (see page 244), Richter is now behind the stick at Dear Irving—a far cry from rotating ladies' nights in 1980s Chicago.

Speaking of Dear Irving, here's a favorite from Tom Richter:

··· PEACE TREATY ···

GARNISH: lemon twist

GLASS: coupe

- 2 ounces Manzanilla sherry
- 1 ounce Vermouth Royale Blanc
- ½ ounce maraschino liqueur
- 2 dashes orange bitters

1. Combine all ingredients in a mixing glass and stir until well chilled.

2. Strain into a chilled coupe and express the twist over the drink by running the peel skin side–down around the rim of the glass and arranging over the cocktail.

Seamstress

339 East 75th Street
New York, NY 10021
(212) 288-8033
seamstressny.com

The entrance to Seamstress is easy to miss unless one knows to look out for the gilded scissors logo. A tiny leather and accessories shop takes up the front of the restaurant, from which point one is led into the large, wood-paneled space. Owned by Steve Laycock, Josh Mazza and Francis Verral of the Gilroy, it's primarily a restaurant offering elevated takes on American comfort food from chef Will Horowitz. But the cocktails from head bartender Pam Wiznitzer, who moved uptown from the Dead Rabbit, are what everyone raves about. Here are two of her standouts:

The name is a play on No Sé, the name of the bar in Antigua, Guatamala where Ilegal Mezcal founder John Rexer first brought attention to the spirit he'd smuggled in from Oaxaca, Mexico.

❖

GARNISH: makrut lime leaf

GLASS: rocks/Old Fashioned

- 1¾ ounces Ilegal Mezcal
- ¾ Aperol
- ¼ ounce Clement Mahina Coco
- 1 ounce lime juice
- ½ ounce pineapple juice
- ¾ ounce lemongrass syrup (1:1 syrup made with a few slices of fresh lemongrass)

Shake all ingredients with ice and strain into the glass over fresh ice. Garnish with lime leaf.

SAXON + PAROLE

316 Bowery
New York, NY 10012
(212) 254-0350
saxonandparole.com

Named for two 19th-century racehorses, Saxon + Parole was mainly presented as an upscale comfort food restaurant when it opened in 2011. However, the bar program, overseen first by Naren Young and now by Masa Urishido, has since drawn its own stable of followers. Here are two of its first-place winners:

··· CELERY GIMLET ···

This drink was created by Naren Young in the fall of 2011.

GARNISH: celery stick and lime wheel
GLASS: rocks/Old Fashioned

- 1½ ounces NY Distilling Dorothy Parker gin
- ¼ ounce Green Chartreuse
- ¼ ounce St-Germain liqueur
- ¾ ounce lime juice
- ½ ounce celery juice (add one cup of diced celery to simple 1:1 recipe, cool and strain)
- ½ ounce lime syrup
- 5 dashes of verjus
- 2 dashes of celery bitters
- pinch of citrus salt

Shake all ingredients with ice and strain into glass over fresh ice. Garnish.

Created by Masa Urushido in fall 2016, this cocktail is a real show-stopper at the bar. While the typical home bartender does not keep fat-washed Scotch and mushroom cordial stocked—never mind black truffles—this drink is a highly-recommended study in luxurious flavor-layering, should the ingredients present themselves.

GARNISH: lemon twist (discard) + freshly shaved black truffle

GLASS: rocks/Old Fashioned

- **2 ounces Chivas Regal 12 Year Scotch, fat-washed with black truffle butter**
- **¼ ounce smoked portobello mushroom cordial**
- **2 dashes of Scrappy's Chocolate bitters**

Stir ingredients with ice until chilled. Strain over freshly carved ice into glass. Garnish.

··· MACE ···

Alphabet City mourned when Louis 649 (see page 245) closed, but rejoiced when Zachary Sharaga and Cocktail Kingdom's Greg Boehm eventually re-opened it as Mace. Head bartender Nico de Soto's wildly imaginative menu is a round-the-world tour of exotic spices, with each cocktail showcasing one ingredient. The bar's namesake cocktail is real stunner, with a dramatic tableside spritz of mace tincture. Though not the easiest thing to replicate at home, here's the recipe for the more adventurous home bartender.

GARNISH: 2 mists of mace tincture

GLASS: coupe

- 1 ounce Linie Aquavit
- 1 ounce Aperol
- ½ ounce rectified fresh orange juice
- ½ ounce fresh beet juice
- ¾ ounce young coconut syrup

Shake all ingredients with ice. Double-strain into the glass. Mist twice with mace tincture.

SLOWLY SHIRLEY

121 West 10th Street, downstairs
(212) 243-2827
slowlyshirley.com

Jim Kearns had long envisioned opening an "everyman kind of cocktail bar" attached to a regular bar, and that's exactly what Slowly Shirley is. The Happiest Hour, located right above it, is known for its 1950s-Hollywood-diner-meets-cocktails concept and its decadent, Instagram-famous burgers—but it's become a huge bridge-and-tunnel scene. Slowly Shirley, where the atmosphere is more akin to an old-school Hollywood nightclub, is "more for people who pay attention to a drink the same way they pay attention to a good dish when eating out," says Kearns. Kearns' cocktails have already received a lot of attention, first in the early days of Pegu Club, then Death & Co and most recently at the bar at the Nomad Hotel. A few of those greatest hits appear on Kearns' menu, though like the décor itself, the drink themes skew more cinematic, with names like Casablanca, The Sun Also Rises, Han Shot First and Five Finger Death Punch. Even better for those who still crave that burger from upstairs? If you order downstairs, they'll bring one down to you.

I asked Kearns for this recipe, because I love a good port cocktail . . .and because you can't beat that name.

❖

GARNISH: cocoa-chile-sugar powder,
orange twist–wrapped straw
GLASS: rocks/Old Fashioned

- 2 dashes Amargo Chuncho
- 2 dashes Bittermen's Hellfire Shrub
- ¼ ounce Tempus Fugit Creme de Cacao
- ½ ounce ruby port
- ½ ounce Pedro Ximenez sherry
- ½ ounce Barbancourt Five Star Rum
- 1½ ounces Cotes du Rhone wine
- orange twist, in the shaker

Shake all ingredients with ice. Strain into a rocks glass over crushed ice. Garnish.

Bar Goto

245 Eldridge Street
(212) 475-4411
bargoto.com

"That's a terrible idea," said no one after Kenta Goto began telling people he was opening his own bar. And in the summer of 2015, the former head bartender at Pegu Club opened Bar Goto on the Lower East Side. The small, modern space is exactly what one might expect from him—clean lines, subtle lighting, exquisitely presented Japanese-inspired cocktails, yummy Japanese-style small plates (including what many consider to be the best wings in town) and a small but excellent whiskey collection on the back bar. Of course with a name like "Goto" he was destined to open the next go-to spot in New York City. The cocktails, such as the Calpico Fizz, Plum Sazerac, Far East Side, Sakura Martini and New Jack City, are such fun to sip; Goto was kind enough to share his recipes for the latter two:

··· NEW JACK CITY ···

GARNISH: gingko leaf
GLASS: coupe or Martini

- 1¼ ounces Japanese plum brandy
- ¾ ounce rye whiskey
- ¾ ounce applejack brandy
- 4 teaspoon red vermouth

1. Combine all ingredients in a mixing glass. Add ice and stir until chilled.

2. Strain into a Martini glass. Garnish with gingko leaf.

GARNISH: cherry blossom

GLASS: Martini or coupe

- 2½ ounces dry sake
- 1 ounce gin

- ¼ teapsoon Maraschino liqueur

1. Combine all ingredients in a mixing glass. Add ice and stir until chilled.

2. Strain into the glass. Garnish with cherry blossom.

PORCHLIGHT

271 11th Avenue
New York, NY 10001
(212) 981-6188
porchlightbar.com

From NYC restaurateur Danny Meyers (Union Square Café, Shake Shack, Gramercy Tavern, etc.) comes this take on southern-casual-meets-high-end cocktails. The remote, westerly location north of the meatpacking district was a bit of a risk, even with its close proximity to the Highline, but one wouldn't know from its consistently lively crowds. The bar's dramatic signature cocktail, the Gun Metal Blue by beverage director Nicholas Bennett, was one of the "it" drinks when the bar opened in 2015 and continues to be a crowd pleaser.

··· GUN METAL BLUE ···

GARNISH: orange coin, overproof rum for lighting on fire

GLASS: coupe

- 1½ ounces Mezcal Vida
- ½ ounce Blue Curaçao
- ¼ ounce peach brandy
- ¾ ounce fresh lime juice
- ¼ ounce bitter cinnamon syrup

1. Shake all ingredients with ice and strain into a chilled coupe.

2. Float the orange coin skin side–down over the drink, careful not to wet the inside.

3. Gently fill coin with a couple of drops of the rum, then light on fire.

— *Spotlight: Mimi Burnham* —

Though Mimi Burnham is relatively new to the current city cocktail scene, she is no rookie. In the 1980s and early '90s, she bartended in some of the city's hottest bars and clubs, including Danceteria. After a 17-year hiatus, she returned to be a part of the cocktail scene.

The USBG (United States Bartending Guild) helped her network for opportunities, and she quickly made connections and friends. Back on the scene, she quickly noticed how varied the education opportunities were for bartenders—a far cry from the old days. And as Burnham says, "There is always something new to learn."

Burnham now divides her time between working as a brand ambassador for Perfect Purée and bartending at Porchlight. She was one of the first bartenders they hired, introduced to the owners by publicist Hanna Lee. Burnham liked their "independent thinking for a corporate spot . . .how genuine and kind the organization is, especially since I'm an older woman. That shows there is no ageism or sexism happening."

Working part time is exactly her speed right now, and the bar is usually quite crowded for most of the evening. "It drains you. Thoroughly." Still, Burnham brings a certain *je ne sais quoi* to her customer approach, always making guests feel at home. "Though you're not in their living room—you're at work." She says she feels grounded by the experience. A witty sense of humor helps. Her advice for a long shift? "Always leave them laughing."

NITECAP

151 Rivington Street
New York, NY 10002
(212) 228-4139
nightcapnyc.com

Some nights you need to end the night with a wallop, and others the mood calls for something lighter. At this underground bar, owned by David Kaplan and Alex Day (of Death & Co) and Natasha David (formerly of Maison Premiere), you can choose either. Or both.

··· DISAPPEARING ACT ···

GARNISH: lemon twist

GLASS: coupe

- 1 ounce Lillet Blanc
- ½ ounce Linie Aquavit
- ½ ounce lemon juice
- ½ ounce simple syrup
- 1 teaspoon Giffard Peche liqueur
- Sparkling wine

1. Shake all ingredients except the bubbly with ice. Strain into the coupe.

2. Top with sparkling wine and garnish.

The Up and Up

116 Macdougal Street
New York, NY 10012
(212) 260-3000
upandupnyc.com

Mesmerizing wallpaper that looks as though it could have been swiped from the set of a Merchant Ivory movie adorns the walls in this small subterranean bar, which used to be the historic West Village beatnik coffeehouse, the Gaslight Café. Opened in 2015 by Matt Piacentini (formerly of the Beagle), it focuses on cocktails with highly unusual flavor combinations. Here is a bittersweet concoction from head bartender Chaim Dauermann:

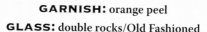

⋯ SCREEN DOOR SLAM ⋯

GARNISH: orange peel
GLASS: double rocks/Old Fashioned

- 2 ounces Maker's Mark bourbon
- 1 ounce vanilla bean–infused Aperol (recipe follows)
- ¼ ounce honey syrup (2:1 honey to water)
- Absinthe (rinse)

1. Stir all ingredients except the absinthe with ice until well chilled.

2. Rinse the glass with absinthe. Strain the drink into the glass over a large format or hand cut cube.

3. Garnish by expressing the orange over the drink before adding.

Vanilla Bean-Infused Aperol

1. Split one fresh vanilla bean down the middle. Leave inside a bottle of Aperol for at least 3 days.

2. Strain the mixture when you are ready to use it, or leave the bean inside the bottle if you prefer.

··· BLACKTAIL RUM & COLA ···

For a bar dedicated to the spirit of Prohibition-era Cuba, a rum & cola variation was essential. But to deconstruct its ingredients and use sparkling wine as the fizz? Utterly brilliant work by Jillian Vose.

GARNISH: lemon twist

GLASS: highball

- 1 dash Orinoco Bitters
- ½ teaspoon Fernet Branca
- ¾ ounce cola syrup
- 1 ounce Bacardi Facundo NEO rum
- 4 ounce Champagne

1. Add all ingredients except Champagne to the glass and stir with ice.

2. Top with Champagne and garnish.

Spotlight: Jack McGarry of The Dead Rabbit and BlackTail

Jack McGarry isn't even 30 yet and he's already considered an industry veteran. When McGarry and Sean Muldoon (his partner from the award-winning Belfast bar The Merchant) came to New York in 2012 to open The Dead Rabbit Grocery and Grog, they had their eyes on the prize: tops on The World's 50 Best Bars list. After only three years, they achieved that goal in 2016. What's more, their nearly one-year-old sister bar BlackTail, a reimagined Prohibition-era Cuba fantasy, is positioned for similar success.

All this sounds a bit pretentious, doesn't it? Never mind world's best—isn't every bar supposed to provide a hospitable, comforting experience, make great drinks and draw repeat visits? Why all the fuss? Yet there truly is something different about spending time at these bars. The staffs at both venues exude a true sense of family, and though it can sometimes be a long wait for a stool or a table, there is no pretense once you're comfortably situated—just extraordinary cocktails and craveworthy food accompanying it. (It doesn't hurt that each venue offers a small amuse drink on the house as a welcome.) In other words, one feels at home, or at least what we wish home resembled. Here, McGarry shares some insight into how it all comes together:

ON THE FORMULA FOR RUNNING A SUCCESSFUL BAR: "The most important starting point of any successful organization is clarity on the why of the business and making sure all of your people are aligned. The Dead Rabbit's why is abundantly clear—we want to bring the Irish Pub into the 21st century. Our people are clear on our expectations and we're even taking additional steps to increase the visibility of our expectations and ensure effective and efficient communication on our short- and long-term goals, keeping all of us accountable. However, it's one thing having clear expectations of your team—that's important, but it has to be followed with religious discipline and focus.

[Sean and I] live the brand and bar. So we have a clear understanding of our why and we're religious about bringing it to life each and every day. These are the two most important aspects of our company. The details and lengths we go to all fall under the umbrella of our why and our obsession with delivery falls under living the brand."

ON THE IDEAL BAR PATRON: "One of the core values of our business is diversity . . .we are all about every single guest, every single time. We don't treat industry insiders any different than industry outsiders. Our guests expect to be looked after, and if we prioritize any guest over another we are not delivering on that fundamental expectation. An ideal guest for us, in terms of character, is someone who is respectful of their surroundings and people in those surroundings . . .our only expectation from our guests is respect."

ON IRISH COFFEE: "For Dead Rabbit, I'd always recommend the Irish Coffee [see page 221]. It's our signature drink and a perfect extension of the concept of bringing the Irish Pub into the 21st century. Most Irish Pubs are terrible venues that have perpetuated the commoditization of the Pub by serving an inferior, unthoughtful product. We're all about challenging the status quo. Being disruptive. The Irish Coffee in most Irish Pubs, and many bars in general, is a terrible, terrible Irish Coffee. As a direct consequence, the Irish Coffee isn't given the credit it deserves. We serve the best Irish Coffee in the world, and to anyone who comes into the bar we strongly recommend ordering it, as it will challenge their misconceptions of the drink and, hopefully, Irish Pubs as a whole."

ON REINVENTING THE CUBA LIBRE FOR BLACKTAIL: "We're obviously emphatic in our execution of Cuban Classics. The preeminent drink would be the Cuba Libre, which we simply call 'Rum and Cola.' Again, the Rum and Cola, similar to the Irish Coffee, is a big standard serve. Many Cuban Bars are the same. Our overarching mission is to create unique concepts that are brought to life with unique guest experiences. So similar to Dead Rabbit, we wanted to challenge the status quo of Cuban Cocktails, and Cuban Bars, being pale imitations of their former selves. Our Rum and Cola recipe is sick! It definitely brings the drink to the next level."

··· THE ARMANDE ···

"I created this cocktail while working at Dear Irving. I wanted a drink that tasted of salted caramel while still being strong and intense. I was inspired by Judi Dench's character Armande in the film *Chocolat*. Armande is a fierce lady who discovers she has a sweeter side upon befriending the owner of a local chocolate shop. My drink is just that: fierce with a touch of confectionary sweetness. It has coconut on the nose and when sipped tastes of caramel, cacao and baking spices with a pinch of savory salt. Afterwards, honey and cinnamon linger on the palate."—*Naomi Leslie*

GARNISH: none

GLASS: rocks/Old Fashioned

- 2 dashes Bittermens Xocolatl mole bitters
- 2 barspoons Tempus Fugit Spirits Crème de Cacao
- 1 ounce Appleton Estate Rare Blend 12-Year Old rum
- 1 ounce Old Forester Signature 100-Proof bourbon
- salt or saline solution, to taste

In order of the ingredients list, build your drink in a rocks glass. Add ice and stir briefly before serving.

This is the BlackTail take on the famous cocktail born at the Hotel Nacional in Havana. Here, Jesse Vida adds more tropical notes with banana and yuzu.

GARNISH: grated nutmeg
GLASS: double rocks/Old Fashioned

- ¾ ounce lime juice
- ½ ounce pineapple juice
- ½ ounce yuzu syrup (this can be purchased online)
- ¼ ounce banana syrup
- ¾ ounce Nacional Biz (¼ ounce each of banana liqueur, Suze Gentiane, and apricot eau de vie)
- 2 ounces white rum

1. Shake all ingredients with ice. Strain into the glass over large ice cubes.

2. Grate nutmeg over the drink and serve.

THE DEAD RABBIT
GROCERY AND GROG

30 Water Street
New York, NY 10004
(646) 422-7906
deadrabbitnyc.com

Jack McGarry masterfully ties together port and Irish whiskey in this fetching concoction.

GARNISH: grated nutmeg

GLASS: double rocks/Old Fashioned

- 3 dashes aromatic bitters (such as Angostura or Peychaud's)
- ¾ ounce lime juice
- ¾ ounce raspberry cordial
- ¾ ounce Graham's LBV Port wine
- ¾ ounce Redbreast 12-Year Irish whiskey
- ¾ ounce Dead Rabbit Jamaican Rum Blend (¼ ounce each of light, gold and dark)

1. Shake all ingredients with ice. Strain into glass over large ice cubes.

2. Grate nutmeg over drink and serve.

··· PSYCHO KILLER ···

The ingredients might have you asking, "qu'est-ce que c'est?" but try it and the last thing you'll want to do is run away.

GARNISH: none

GLASS: Nick & Nora/small coupe

- 2 dashes absinthe
- ¾ ounce Campari, infused with coco nibs
- ½ ounce crème de cacao
- ½ ounce Giffard Banane liqueur
- 2 ounces Redbreast 12-Year Irish whiskey

Stir all ingredients with ice until chilled. Strain into glass.

SEASONAL IMBIBING

New York City has beautiful seasons, and nothing quite compares to watching them from inside a bar. Still, there are plenty of good excuses to head outside—or at least to a different bar. Here are some of the best ways to sip through the seasons in the city.

"WHEN IT'S 100 DEGREES IN NEW YORK,
IT'S 72 IN LOS ANGELES. WHEN ITS 30 DEGREES
IN NEW YORK, IN LOS ANGELES IT'S STILL 72.
HOWEVER, THERE ARE 6 MILLION INTERESTING
PEOPLE IN NEW YORK, AND ONLY 72
IN LOS ANGELES."

—*Neil Simon*

Rooftop Bars

One can never grow weary of viewing the city from above, and there is an incomparable thrill to raising a glass over our wondrous skyline. But it's far more enjoyable when what's in the glass is as good as the view itself. Some rooftop bars think they can get away with scenery alone, and that drink prices should match the privilege of the experience. Here are some good ones that are worth the climb (or the extensive wait for an elevator).

The Empire Rooftop at the Empire Hotel

44 West 63rd Street
New York, NY 10023
(212) 265-7400
empirehotelnyc.com

Obviously warmer seasons invite the most rooftop imbibing, but this stylish Lincoln Center lounge is equipped with both indoor and outdoor seating, as well as a working fireplace. You haven't lived till you've watched a New York snowfall from a high vantage point. This place serves classic cocktails with a few of the their own twists. It's the perfect location to gaze at the skyline and declare, "There is something in the New York air that makes sleep useless," as Simone de Beauvoir once did.

Bar 54 at the Hyatt Times Square

135 West 45th Street
New York, NY 10036
(646) 364-1234
timessquarehyatt.com

Like the Empire, this rooftop bar also features indoor seating. However, they take it up a notch with what they refer to as Bubbles—"igloo-like" heated seating areas where one can take in the glorious views from 54 stories up, making this one of the highest lounges in the city. An added bonus, the cocktail program was originally designed by Julie Reiner of Clover Club (see page 98), so at least the sky-high pricing won't give you altitude sickness.

I f you can't make it to Bar 54, at least you can make a Bermuda Beer Run.

GARNISH: lemon wheel and cherry flag
GLASS: highball

- 1½ ounces Gosling's Dark Rum
- ½ ounce Angostura Amaro
- ½ ounce lemon juice
- ½ ounce Carpano Antica
- ½ ounce simple syrup
- Bronx Pale Ale beer

1. Shake all ingredients except for beer with ice. Strain into a highball glass with fresh ice.

2. Top with beer. Garnish by spearing a cocktail pick through the lemon and cherry and laying over rim of glass.

"MANHATTAN HAS BEEN COMPELLED TO EXPAND SKYWARD BECAUSE OF THE ABSENCE OF ANY OTHER DIRECTION IN WHICH TO GROW."

—*E.B. White from This is New York*

ROOF AT PARK SOUTH
125 East 27th Street
New York, NY 10016
(212) 204-5222
roofatparksouth.com

This rooftop bar is only open seasonally, but it isn't as swoungey (swank + loungey) as the previous two. In other words, it's more of a down-to-earth experience for drinking up high. Guests sit at barstools arranged around communal tables, sipping unfussy riffs on classic cocktails from beverage director Ted Kilpatrick. Bites also skew toward pub casual, with options such as pizzas, burgers and hummus platters. A Duke's Martini with a side of caviar seems a tad out of place, although with this unobstructed view, it's forgivable—especially if someone with a traveling expense account is paying.

BOOKMARKS AT THE LIBRARY HOTEL
299 Madison Avenue
New York, NY 10017
(212) 204-5419
libraryhotel.com

With its wraparound terrace, this all-season, semi-outdoor bar in midtown is a mere fourteen floors up. However, what sets it apart is the library-chic décor and imaginative literary-themed cocktail list. Relax into a leather wing-backed chair with a Dante's Inferno or a Pulitzer (made with Dorothy Parker gin, obviously) or a Tequila Mockingbird. Where else can you sip a bookish drink, snack on some sliders and feel right at home quoting Ezra Pound: "And New York is the most beautiful city in the world? It is not far from it. No urban night is like the night there. . .Squares after squares of flame, set up and cut into the aether. Here is our poetry, for we have pulled down the stars to our will."

IDES AT WYTHE HOTEL
80 Wythe Avenue
Brooklyn, NY 11249
(718) 460-8006
wythehotel.com

It's all fine and dandy to sip drinks on a Manhattan roof, but the best way to see the skyline is from across the river. The lines for this bar at the edge of Williamsburg can get long, but it's worth the wait, especially if timed around sunset. Cocktails are well made and affordable (another reason to leave the main island) and the food selection is varied enough to be more interesting than most roof lounges, with offerings to satisfy all dietary needs.

IF YOU LIKE PIÑA COLADAS

"Stop calling it a 'disco drink.' If you go anywhere else [outside of the cocktail industry bubble] it's just as revered as the rest of them." When Giuseppe González opened the Suffolk Arms, it was important to him to offer a real Piña Colada, and that meant there had to be a blender behind the bar. He grew up in the Bronx, where coladas outsell almost any other type of cocktail. "Think about the Hennessy Colada, a popular drink in Washington Heights that unites both blacks and Puerto Ricans. They go through like 20 cases of booze a week to make these slushies . . .When I wanted to put [a colada] on the Pegu Club menu, Audrey Saunders said, 'Joey's trying to bring back the Piña Colada.' I'm not trying to bring it back, it's in my DNA." Modern-day bartenders keep trying to elevate the recipe by subbing the Coco Lopez for something less fattening, or using a nitro machine instead of a blender. What everyone discovers is that it's better not to try and fix what ain't broke—it needs to be creamy, it needs to be a little sweet and it should be made in a blender. "Don't judge people by what they drink. Do they like it? That's the important thing," says González. "'Disco drink?' Nah. It's a beach drink."

SUFFOLK ARMS

269 East Houston Street
New York, NY 10002
(212) 475-0400
suffolkarms.com

Giuseppe González's East Village pub is a love letter to New York City culture. His Improved Piña Colada is one of its most popular orders all year round, but especially on a steamy day.

THE RUM HOUSE

228 West 47th Street
New York, NY 10036
(646) 490-6924
therumhousenyc.com

The Rum House also makes one of the city's best Piña Colada variations, its name is a direct homage to the famous song by Rupert Holmes. It's a lovely thing to order in the theater district after being caught in the rain. Remember, what you do after midnight is your own business.

··· IMPROVED PIÑA COLADA ···

GARNISH: orange slice

GLASS: hurricane

- 2 ounces spiced rum
- 1½ ounces pineapple juice
- 2 ounces Coco Lopez
- ½ ounce passionfruit purée
- Campari (float)

1. Blend all the ingredients except the Campari with ice in a blender until smooth. Pour into glass.

2. Using the back of a barspoon, pour about ¼ ounce of the Campari over the spoon to float over the drink. Garnish with orange slice.

··· THE ESCAPE ···

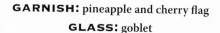

GARNISH: pineapple and cherry flag

GLASS: goblet

- 2 ounces El Dorado Dark Rum
- 1 ounce pineapple juice
- 1 ounce Coco Lopez
- ¾ ounce sweet vermouth (float)

1. Shake all ingredients except vermouth vigorously with ice. Note: The bar has no blender, but go ahead and blend it if you have one.

2. Strain into the glass if shaken; pour the whole lot in if blended. Float the vermouth over the top. Garnish.

MOTHER'S RUIN

18 Spring Street
New York, NY 10012
no phone
mothersruinnyc.com

Sitting by the water or viewing the city from above is fun on a hot summer day in the city, but so is sitting in a bar with big open windows and refreshing cold drinks. Opened in 2011 by Richard Knapp and T.J. Lynch, this Nolita bar and comfort food restaurant is one of the few spots open every day at 11 AM. In the summer, they are known for their slushy menu and icy drinks like this one from Lynch.

··· OVERSIZED TOOL ···

GARNISH: 3 Luxardo cherries

GLASS: Collins

- ¾ ounce light rum
- ¾ ounce amber rum
- ¾ ounce Luxardo maraschino cherry syrup (from the can)
- 1 ounce fresh lime

1. Shake all ingredients with ice. Strain into Collins glass filled with crushed ice.

2. Top with more crushed ice. Garnish with the cherries threaded on a skewer.

Spring and Summer By the Water

Do you prefer your libations at sea level? Then come aboard these floating bars and riverside taverns that open in the warmer months. While there are bars everywhere by the water, these ones have the best actual drinks. I recommend checking their websites for hours and updates, as well as planning on a bit of a wait—especially after 5 P.M.—since most of them do not accept reservations.

GRAND BANKS

Pier 25
Hudson River Park
New York, NY 10013
(212) 660-6312
grandbanks.org

This oyster bar and seafood restaurant can be found on the deck of a historic fishing boat, which remains docked at the pier. What it lacks in décor, it makes up for in quality drinks, fresh ingredients and focused preparation. Even with the buildings in the distance, floating on the water feels like a temporary escape from the city heat.

ROCKAWAY BEACH SURF CLUB

302 Beach 87th Street
Rockaway Beach, NY 11693
no phone
rockawaybeachsurfclub.com

I don't recommend hitching a ride to get to Rock Rock Rockaway Beach, but you just haven't experienced summer in the city without a trip to the seaside. There are tons of good joints along the boardwalk, but this one serves some of the best food—incredible tacos, a whole noodle list and fresh juices to boot. While there are only a couple of cocktails on the menu, they're ex-

actly what they should be, including a really fun, slightly less caloric Piña Colada that uses quality coconut rum instead of Coco Lopez and Gosling's dark rum. It's a bit of a trek to get out here, but good things come to those who schlep.

Fornino at Brooklyn Bridge Park

Pier 6
Brooklyn, NY 11201
(718) 422-1107
fornino.com

Manhattan skyline across the water, fresh wood-fired pizzas, well made cocktails that don't break the bank, *and* it's technically a rooftop bar? You're welcome.

Jade Island

Richmond Shopping Center
2845 Richmond Avenue
Staten Island, NY 10314
(718) 761-8080
jadeislandstaten.com

Jade Island opened in 1972 in the middle of Staten Island just as the first tiki craze was saying its final alohas. This Chinese restaurant and lounge is decked out in full old-school tiki glory, with thatched hut roofs over its booths, waterfalls, palm trees, ukulele music and servers in Hawaiian shirts. If you're looking for so-phisticated drinks with ingredients like amaro and gentian, you've come to the wrong place—not much has changed in 45 years of busi-ness. But if you want to share a pu pu platter with a decent Mai Tai, Blue Hawaiian or something served in a hollowed-out pineapple, you're exactly where you need to be. It's especially refreshing after a breezy summer ferry ride, though to get there you'll need to travel inland a bit. Check the website for directions.

Fall and Winter

"LIVING IN CALIFORNIA ADDS TEN YEARS
TO A MAN'S LIFE. AND THOSE EXTRA TEN YEARS
I'D LIKE TO SPEND IN NEW YORK."

—*Harry Ruby*

As the temperatures start to drop in New York, there are far better things to drink than vodka and lime. Most bars will serve toddies or hot buttered somethings to restore feeling in our cheeks, so it's really hard to go wrong. When the bitter wind whips through the streets and lashes our chilly limbs, these warming drinks around town really soothe our souls.

ANALOGUE AT ANALOGUE

19 West 8th Street
New York, NY 10011
(212) 432-0200
analoguenyc.com

"The Analogue was our first drink on the menu. When we opened, we wanted a bourbon-focused drink that was good for the cooler fall weather in New York [Analogue opened in November 2013]. When I tasted it I said to our bartender, 'Wow, if I could taste our bar that would be it! What should we call it?' And the response was, 'Well if that's what it is, then call it Analogue.' And it's been on our menu ever since day one."—*co-owner Jesse Wilson*

··· ANALOGUE ···

GARNISH: lemon twist

GLASS: rocks/Old Fashioned

- 1 ounce Four Roses Bourbon
- 1½ ounces dark rum
- ½ ounce Velvet Falernum
- ¼ ounce Domaine de Canton ginger liqueur
- ¼ ounce St Elizabeth Allspice dram
- 3 dashes Angostura bitters

Stir all ingredients with ice. Strain into the glass over a large format ice cube. Garnish.

Miner created this appley autumn favorite when he was head bartender at the now-departed JakeWalk in Brooklyn. Luckily, you can still order one from him at Long Island Bar in Boerum Hill, and he was kind enough to share the recipe to make at home.

GARNISH: dusting of nutmeg, freshly ground
GLASS: coupe

- 1½ ounces Laird's bonded applejack
- ¾ ounce cinnamon syrup (recipe follows)
- ¾ ounce fresh lemon juice
- ½ ounce Galliano L'Authentico
- 2 dashes St. Elizabeth's all spice dram

1. Combine all ingredients in a cocktail shaker with ice. Shake to chill and combine.

2. Double strain into a chilled cocktail glass. Garnish with a dusting of freshly ground nutmeg.

Cinnamon Syrup

In a small saucepan, combine:

- 16 ounces water
- 16 ounces granulated sugar
- 6 cinnamon sticks

Let simmer for about 15 minutes. Strain. Allow syrup to cool before using.

The Duke of Suffolk at Suffolk Arms

Irish coffee for tea drinkers! This next level downtown cocktail is from the deliciously twisted mind of the boy from the Bronx, Giuseppe González, who was kind enough to share his recipe.

Pleasant Demise at Bonnie Vee

17 Stanton Street
New York, NY 10002
(917) 639-3352
bonnievee.com

This cocktail by owner Nino Cirabisi showcases two tastes from seasonal fruits that taste great together—pear as a liqueur and pomegranate in the homemade grenadine.

The Late Late Bar

159 East Houston Street
New York, NY 10002
(646) 861-3342
thelatelate.com

For most pubs around town, cocktails are an afterthought. But the staff at this lively East Village Irish pub pays as much attention to their cocktail program as they do their beer and whiskey. Bartender Seth Allen's Wild Hot Toddy has a touch of vanilla whiskey to lend it a wintry richness.

GARNISH: none

GLASS: glass mug

- 1¼ ounces Hendrick's or Ford's Gin

- Hot sweet tea (brew English Breakfast and Earl Grey Tea, sweetened with 3:1 simple syrup)
- Whipped cream

Build the drink in the mug by adding the gin, then stir with the hot sweet tea. Top with fresh cream float.

GARNISH: sprig of fresh thyme

GLASS: coupe

- 1½ ounces London Dry Gin
- ½ ounce St. George Spiced Pear liqueur
- ½ ounce fresh lemon juice
- ½ ounce Spiced Grenadine (recipe follows)
- 4 dashes Peychaud's Bitters

Add all ingredients to a cocktail shaker with ice. Shake vigorously and double strain into a chilled coupe glass. Garnish with a sprig of fresh thyme.

Spiced Grenadine

- 3 cups 100% pomegranate juice
- 3 cinnamon sticks
- ½ ounce whole clove
- ½ ounce pomegranate molasses
- 3 cups white sugar
- peel of 1 orange

1. In a saucepan over medium heat, simmer 1½ cups of pomegranate juice with the cinnamon sticks, orange peel and cloves until the liquid is reduced by half.

2. Take off heat, strain, add the remaining 1½ cups of pomegranate juice, molasses and sugar.

3. Return to heat and stir until sugar is completely dissolved. Let cool before using.

··· THE APPLE TODDY ···

Julie Reiner reimagines this classic New York drinks for her Brooklyn bar. Cinnamon-apple tea gives it an extra hug of flavor.

GARNISH: long lemon peel with 4 cloves
GLASS: glass mug

- 2 ounces Calvados or applejack
- 1 teaspoon maple syrup
- 3 ounces hot cinnamon-apple tea (made from brewed tea blend)

1. Fill the mug with hot water to keep it warm.

2. Using a vegetable peeler, cut a long spiral of lemon peel in a circular motion while rotating the lemon. Pierce the peel with the cloves and set aside.

3. Empty the water from the mug. Add the apple brandy and syrup, then stir in the hot tea. Garnish with the peel.

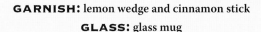

··· WILD HOT TODDY ···

GARNISH: lemon wedge and cinnamon stick

GLASS: glass mug

- 1 ounce Wild Turkey 101 Rye
- ½ ounce Crown Royal Vanilla whiskey
- ½ ounce honey syrup
- loose black tea blend of choice, such as English Breakfast or Earl Grey, placed in single serving tea ball

1. Add the whiskeys and syrup to the glass and stir.

2. Add the tea ball and top with hot water. Allow the tea to brew 3 minutes, then stir and remove tea ball.

3. Garnish and serve.

HOLIDAYS IN NEW YORK CITY

Around of "Fairytale" at a bar on Christmas Eve belongs on any NYC bucket list. Real New Yorkers love spending holidays in town because we can reclaim the city for ourselves—the frenetic pace slows down a bit, the streets are relatively empty, traffic eases and there's a quiet seat at our busy local favorites. The bars and restaurants that remain open provide a refuge for those who prefer to be out during Thanksgiving, Christmas, Easter, New Year's Day and the many three-day weekends during summer. Here are some of the best ways to drink in the big holidays and happenings around town, and recipes shared by some favorite destinations.

"THE BUILDINGS ARE SHIMMERING VERTICALITY,
A GOSSAMER VEIL, A FESTIVE SCENE-PROP
HANGING THERE AGAINST THE BLACK SKY
TO DAZZLE, ENTERTAIN, AMAZE."

—*Frank Lloyd Wright*

CHRISTMAS

Since 2014 and 2015, respectively, popular East Village bars Mace and Boilermaker have shut down regular operations to transform into the pop-up wonderlands Miracle on 9th Street and Sippin' Santa's Surf Shack. Thanks to Greg Boehm and the creative minds behind Cocktail Kingdom, these festive grottos were so successful in their first outings that they are now a global phenomenon, taking place as far away as Athens, Greece. Lines to get in can snake around the block, but it's worth enduring the cold to sip a Yippee Ki Yay Mother F****r! out of a mug shaped like Santa's pants. Most of the drinks are be too complicated to replicate at home, thanks to their special house ingredients, but Cocktail Kingdom was kind enough to share a couple of their recipes for you to deck your own halls.

MIRACLE ON 9TH STREET (A.K.A. MACE)

649 East 9th Street
New York, NY 10009

From the Miracle bars, these recipes are courtesy of head bartender Nico de Soto:

SURFIN' SANTA'S SURF SHACK (A.K.A. BOILERMAKER)

13 First Avenue
New York, NY 10003
(212) 995-5400

Sippin' Santa's Surf Shack is a tiki fantasy, where one imagines Mr. and Mrs. Kringle would like to relax on December 26.

··· CHRISTMAPOLITAN ···

GARNISH: red ribbon tied around the stem of glass
GLASS: coupe

- 1½ ounces vodka
- 1 ounce St-Germain liqueur
- 1 ounce spiced cranberry sauce (good use of holiday leftovers!)
- ½ ounce fresh lime juice
- 2 dashes fig bitters

Shake all ingredients with ice. Strain into decorated coupe.

··· . . . AND A PARROT IN A PALM TREE ···

BY PAUL MCGEE OF LOST LAKE IN CHICAGO

GARNISH: cinnamon stick and orchid, straw

GLASS: Beachbum Berry's Latitude 29 coconut vessel, or a tiki mug

- 1½ ounces tequila reposado
- ½ ounce mezcal joven
- ½ ounce Pierre Ferrand Dry Curaçao
- 2 ounce spiced coconut syrup (make Spiced Syrup from page 233 with coconut water instead of regular water)
- 1 ounce lime juice

Shake all ingredients with ice. Pour into glass over crushed ice. Top with more crushed ice and garnish.

LOCL AT THE NYLO
HOTEL
222 West 77th Street
New York, NY 10024
(212) 651-3319

Remember that dream in which you sipped a cocktail from a snow globe? Oh, that was just me? Well, at LOCL it can be yours too. During the holiday season, take a load off from shopping and the cattle call of tree-gazing tourists in midtown, relax at this loungey hotel bar and order the Shakespeare's Globe cocktail. If that's too jingle bell–centric, try Puck's Shadow, with a toast-your-own marshmallow garnish! Here's an adaptation of Cody Goldstein's recipe:

··· LADY MACBETH'S SECRET RECIPE ···

This toddy uses sparkling wine as an extra topping, bringing ultimate holiday festiveness!

❖

GARNISH: lemon twist

GLASS: snowman or other decorative mug

- 1½ ounces Knappogue Castle 12-Year Single Malt Irish Whiskey
- 3 ounces Apple Cider
- ½ ounce Earl Grey Syrup (make standard 1:1 simple syrup with 3 teabags, and strain)
- ½ ounce lemon juice
- hot water
- 2 ounces sparkling wine

1. Add whiskey, cider, syrup and lemon juice to the mug and stir.

2. Top with hot water, leaving about half an inch or so in the mug and stir again.

3. Top with sparkling wine and garnish.

St. Patrick's Day

New York has one of the biggest St. Patrick's Day celebrations in North America, but typically this is a day most real New Yorkers duck for cover to escape the flood of green beer and over-served amateurs singing "Danny Boy" off key. There are a few reliable refuges around town, or you can make some spectacular Irish cocktails for an at-home celebration.

The Dead Rabbit Grocery and Grog (for more bar info, see page 174)

The Dead Rabbit is open from late morning into late evening, serving full Irish breakfast, corned beef and cabbage and other delicacies. Apart from a properly pulled Guinness, they also offer a magnificent Irish coffee. Just as toast or a good sandwich always tastes better when someone else makes it, this recipe is best consumed at the bar. However, for when you can't get to Water Street (there's a song in there somewhere), here's how to make it at home:

Sweet Afton

30-09 34th Street
Astoria, NY 11103
(718) 777.2570
sweetaftonbar.com

"Sweet Afton's owner, Ruairi Curtin, is an immigrant from Cork—but we're not an Irish bar, per se. We like to incorporate subtle Irish touches into our drinks. Teeling Irish Whiskey is a fantastic Irish whiskey newcomer, and sherry [specifically its barrel finish] is quite popular with older Irish folks. The Irish made New York City what it is. The borough of Queens, where our bar is located, was built by the Irish. New York's cocktail culture wouldn't be what it is if it weren't for the thousands of Irish bars that dot the city."—*Mike Di Tota*

··· IRISH COFFEE ···

GARNISH: nutmeg, freshly grated

GLASS: glass mug

- 1½ ounces Irish whiskey (bar uses Clontarf blended)
- 4 ounces brewed coffee, mixed with rich syrup to taste (usually about a teaspoon)
- fresh whipped cream

1. Warm the glass by adding hot water to it and let sit for 30 seconds. Pour out the water and fill with the whiskey, then the coffee mixture and stir.

2. Top with whipped cream, then grate the nutmeg directly over the top. Sláinte!

··· PENNY LANE ···

GARNISH: brandied cherries

GLASS: coupe

- 1½ ounces Teeling Irish Whiskey
- 1 ounce simple syrup
- ½ ounce Oloroso sherry
- ½ ounce fresh lemon juice
- ¼ ounce Cappelletti
- ¼ ounce Luxardo Maraschino liqueur
- 2 dashes orange blossom water
- 2 dashes grapefruit bitters

Add all the ingredients to a shaker and fill with ice. Shake and strain into a chilled coupe. Garnish with a skewer of brandied cherries.

Memorial Day

Memorial Day weekend in America is considered the official summer kickoff holiday. In New York City, it coincides with Fleet Week, an annual celebration welcoming Sailors, Marines and members of the Coast Guard who have been deployed overseas. Fleet Week began in San Diego in 1935 and has become a tradition in other ports of call, such as San Francisco and Fort Lauderdale. In New York it is always timed as a lead-up to Memorial Day, beginning with a flotilla of vessels in the harbor along the Hudson River and continuing with military demonstrations all over the city throughout the week. Venues around town participate with their own events at various piers, monuments and other locales, including drink specials for those with military I.D. It's an excellent time to toast members of these services (encouraged even when it's not Fleet Week); if you encounter them, buy them a drink!

One of my all-time favorite cocktails is Remember the Maine, an especially fitting drink for Memorial Day weekend. Bartender and author Charles H. Baker created the drink in the 1930s to commemorate the U.S.S. Maine, an American ship that exploded in 1898 in Havana Harbor while assisting Cuba in its War of Independence against Spain. "Remember the Maine, to hell with Spain!" was the cry of American protesters during the Cuban Revolution of 1933.

GARNISH: lemon twist

GLASS: coupe

- 1½ ounces rye whiskey
- ¾ sweet vermouth
- barspoon of Cherry Heering liqueur
- dash of absinthe
- dash of Peychaud's bitters

Stir all ingredients (stir clockwise in direction of the tide, a tip from author Philip Greene) with ice until well chilled. Strain into chilled coupe glass. Garnish.

Independence Day

Many city residents choose to celebrate their rights to life, liberty and the pursuit of happiness by getting the heck out of dodge. But here's a self-evident truth: this one of the best weeks to stay in town—the city is so emptied out that anything is possible (including bar seats at Dead Rabbit, BlackTail, PDT, Death & Co and other popular bars). Fireworks celebrations take place over the East River, and though the crowds are enormous, one can also view the spectacle from up high on a rooftop or terrace—ideally on the east side and east-facing parts of Brooklyn and Queens. My suggestion is to find a friend with roof access and bring libations, such as one of the flask drinks on pages 90-93. You can also whip up some boozy summer slushies!

Here's a summery recipe from T.J. Lynch of Mother's Ruin. Adjust measurements according to how many drinks you need!

GARNISH: lemon twist and fresh mint sprigs
GLASS: highball or Solo cup

- 1½ parts tequila blanco
- ¾ parts lemon juice
- 1 part fresh peach
- plenty of fresh mint sprigs and a few for garnishes
- several dashes Angostura bitters (2 dashes per individual cocktail)

Add all ingredients to a blender with crushed ice and blend until smooth. Pour into glasses. Garnish.

Halloween

New York City hosts a good Halloween. Besides the legendary Greenwich Village Halloween parade and the local processions in various neighborhoods across the city, creative decorations adorn windows and storefronts all over town. Certain cocktail bars get into the spirit too. At Leyenda (see page 101), the bar opens early for Diá de los Muertos face-painting (recently done by industry stylist Renée Serra) and Ivy Mix's special pumpkin Margaritas. One of the perennial favorite fall/winter cocktails at Leyenda is the Headless Horseman by bartender Ryan Liloa, which somehow manages to be both blended and flaming, and arrives in a skull mug.

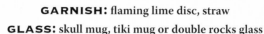

··· HEADLESS HORSEMAN ···

GARNISH: flaming lime disc, straw

GLASS: skull mug, tiki mug or double rocks glass

- 1½ ounces unaged cachaça
- ¾ ounce orange juice
- 1½ ounces pumpkin syrup (1:1 simple syrup with a cup of pumpkin purée, strained)
- ½ ounce allspice dram
- ¾ ounce cinnamon bark syrup
- 1½ ounces coconut blend (1:1 combination of Coco Lopez and coconut milk)
- ¾ ounce lime juice
- overproof 151 rum

1. Blend all ingredients with ice in a blender. Pour into mug or glass over ice.

2. Set the lime disc skin side–down over the drink, fill with rum and light on fire. Sip through straw.

Don't know about you, but I have always found clowns terrifying. They disturb me so much that I worry I've developed a real prejudice against all clowns! But even I can get behind bartender David Nurmi's delicious Mutiny of Clowns cocktail (another Halloween-tastic flaming drink), which was a favorite at the now departed JakeWalk bar in Carroll Gardens.

GARNISH: flaming orange disc
(hey, you're getting some practice by now!)
GLASS: rocks/Old Fashioned

- ¾ ounce Cruzan Blackstrap rum
- ¾ ounce Cynar (original recipe)
- ¾ ounce fresh lime juice
- ½ ounce ginger syrup (1:1 simple syrup made with ¾ cup fresh ginger, sliced into rounds and strained)
- ¼ ounce demerara syrup
- overproof 151 rum

1. Add all ingredients except 151 rum to a tin. Add ice and shake vigorously for 10 seconds.

2. Double strain into a chilled rocks glass with no rocks. Place the orange disc skin side–down on top of the drink, effectively creating a little dish to hold the 151. (Be careful not to dunk the cheek into the drink otherwise it won't ignite.)

3. Drop the 151 in the dish and light on fire! (Make sure the fire goes out before you sip!)

THANKSGIVING

Thanksgiving is one of those occasions where one half expects a bale of tumbleweed to blow down Fifth Avenue—it is *that* quiet. With fewer cocktail bars open for business, this is a good time to entertain at home with family or throw a Friendsgiving (in my house it is a bit of both). Confession time: I'm a hopeless bartender because I've never mastered the art of chatting and properly mixing drinks simultaneously. So instead of rudely shushing guests while I attempt to concentrate on measurements, I make punch. Not only is something served in a punchbowl relatively simple to batch up and maintain, it's festive, welcoming and makes a pretty centerpiece. This is a good recipe to use not only for Thanksgiving, but any festive fall or winter occasion, including Christmas and New Years.

··· THE SPICY STANDISH ···

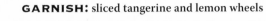

GARNISH: sliced tangerine and lemon wheels
GLASS: punch bowl, small rocks glasses or teacups for serving

- Four 12-ounce bottles of pear cider (2 large-format bottles, if necessary)
- 375 ml brandy
- 175 ml (about ¾ cup) aged rum
- Two 12-ounce bottles ginger beer (the spicier the better)
- ⅓ cup spiced syrup (recipe follows)
- Several dashes of sweet-spicy bitters (try Dale DeGroff's Pimento Bitters, Bitterman's Burlesque or good ol' Peychaud's)

1. If you can, freeze a small bowl or coffee mug of water overnight to make a giant ice dome; this will keep the drink chilled but dilute it less than regular ice. Large ice spheres or cubes also work.

2. Add all the liquids into a punch bowl and give it a good stir.

3. Add sliced fruit and arrange to alternate the colors. Just before guests are due to arrive, add the ice. Ladle away!

Spiced Syrup

- 1 cup water
- 1 cup demerara sugar
- 3 cinnamon sticks
- 5 cloves
- 5 dried allspice berries
- 3 cardamom pods

Heat all ingredients in a saucepan over low heat, until sugar dissolves and mixture coats the back of a wooden spoon. Let cool and strain out solids.

New Year's Eve

I might sound like a curmudgeon here, but New Years Eve in the city is best viewed from the inside. Times Square is not the only zoo—it's amateur hour just about everywhere, and it's hard to find a venue that doesn't insist on an inflated prix fixe menu worth splurging on. My advice? Have a ball drop party. Just gather up some people and watch the thing on TV instead of standing in the cold in a giant, heaving crowd without restroom access. Or worse, sticking it out in a bar next to someone who can't handle their Martinis. Make it a potluck, cook a spread or order in some nibbles. You'll of course want some bubbly on hand for the big moment; have at least a bottle each of red and white wine, and some beer (your guests will bring other bottles unless they're total heathens). Set out a few spirits, mixers and bitters and allow guests to make their own drinks!

That said, you're still going to need a sparkling punch. Here's my favorite holiday recipe, with a festive red hue. Its name comes from *Good King Wenceslas.*

———

"I'M NOT A DRINKER—MY BODY
WILL NOT TOLERATE SPIRITS. I
HAD TWO MARTINIS ON NEW
YEAR'S EVE AND I TRIED TO
HIJACK AN ELEVATOR AND FLY IT
TO CUBA."

—*Woody Allen*

GARNISH: sliced, fresh seasonal fruit and berries of your choice

GLASS: punch bowl

- 2 750-ml bottles of sparkling wine, such as Cava or Prosecco
- 375 ml (half bottle) aged rum or Cognac
- 6 ounces orange liqueur
- 4 ounces (add more to taste) Hibiscus Syrup (recipe follows, though you can find them in stores)
- several dashes Peychaud's bitters

1. Don't forget to freeze a small bowl overnight to make one giant ice cube for the punch, or just freeze your big ice spheres.

2. Stir all the liquids in a punch bowl. Add ice and fresh fruit to dress it up. Ladle into cups and enjoy your company!

Hibiscus Syrup

- 1 cup water
- ½ cup dried hibiscus flowers or 6 bags of hibiscus tea (remove from bags)
- 1 stick cinnamon
- 5 whole cloves
- 5 allspice berries
- 1 vanilla pod, split
- ¾ cup granulated or demerara sugar

1. Add the water, hibiscus and spices to a small pot and bring to boil. When it has come to a full boil, remove from heat and let the flowers steep in the liquid for 15 to 20 minutes.

2. Strain the flowers out of the liquid and return it to the pot with the sugar. Heat it to a boil again while stirring to dissolve the sugar.

3. Simmer until the mixture gets syrupy, another few minutes. Allow to cool before using. Stores for about 10 days in the fridge in a sealed container.

PAST VS. PRESENT

Gone, but Not Forgotten

A good bar is such a cherished part of the city that it's like family. Sadly, so many factors—rent increases, poor business decisions, structural calamities, greedy landlords, corporate remodeling or simply time itself—often force them to close before their time. We've lost too many of our favorite watering holes over the years; indeed, as of this writing, the historic Bull and Bear and Peacock Alley bars in the Waldorf Astoria are closing. The building is being gutted for condos, and whether the bars will open again remains to be seen. This section details a few others whose last call has made a lasting impact.

"Yet, as only New Yorkers know, if you can get through the twilight, you'll live through the night."

— *Dorothy Parker*

THE STORK CLUB

In its heyday, the Stork Club was considered one of the most elegant joints in town. With its VIP Cub Room, the windowless venue ("Isn't this a lovely room? What a clever name, where the elite meet," said Bette Davis in *All About Eve*) became the most exclusive celebrity hangout in town, attracting such guests as Joe DiMaggio, Marilyn Monroe, Cary Grant, Lucille Ball and Desi Arnaz, Sophia Loren, Elizabeth Taylor, Jackie Gleason, Frank Sinatra, Ernest Hemingway and dozens of politicians. Owned by Oklahoma-born bootlegger Sher-

man Billingsley, it was originally located on West 58th Street from 1929 to 1931 before a Prohibition raid forced it to reopen on East 51st off of Fifth Avenue. Gossip columnist and regular Walter Winchell would record its goings on for eager readers, and the club even launched its own live TV program from 1950 to 1955, during which Billingsley would interview celebrity guests amid Martinis and cigarette smoke from his "home" in the Cub Room. The Stork Club was famous for its cutting-edge menu designs—most notably covers by the graphic artist Albert Dorne in the 1940s and Paul Rand, who illustrated the famous cover of the 1945 bar book by Lucius Beebe. Though it was one of the few venues open on Sunday nights and through the summer months, it closed in 1965 when clubs of its kind fell out of fashion. Its demise is considered the official end of the classic New York nightlife era.

The Oak Room/Oak Bar

Two of the most opulent masterpieces of the city are the Plaza Hotel's ornate, German renaissance restaurant and adjacent bar with intricately carved wooden columns. Among its many cinematic appearances, it's where Cary Grant's character is kidnapped in the 1959 Alfred Hitchcock film *North by Northwest*, where Dudley Moore went on quippy benders in 1981's *Arthur* and where Al Pacino tangoed with Gabriel Anwar in *Scent of a Woman* in 1992. The Oak Room only allowed men (it was even called The Men's Bar prior to Prohibition) until 1969, when feminist Betty Friedan led a protest by the National Organization for Women for the bar to allow female guests. This temple of city grandeur is where politicians, celebrities and top business people held their Martini power lunches, and the bar was one of the most spectacular spots in the city to sit with a burger and a Manhattan—if you could stand all the smoke.

The Oak Bar/Room endured many management disasters over the years, but closed in 2004 when the Plaza went condo. In 2011, a disorganized attempt at re-opening forced it to shutter again within months, and currently it is only available for private parties. Luckily, the elegant Palm Court in the lobby has been back in business since 2015, please change to "serving a decent cocktail selection, though under exceedingly bright lights.

Grange Hall

Though it was founded in the early '90s, Grange Hall in the West Village felt like it had been there since the 1930s. As historian David Wondrich pointed out, "It was where people went for classic cocktails if they couldn't afford the Rainbow Room." It was a throwback to a bygone era, a real saloon, complete with live jazz and Depression-era-in-the-heartland fare like succotash. Bartender Del Pedro (who now owns Tooker

Alley in Brooklyn) was one of its longtime bartenders, serving drinks that were hard to find anywhere in town at the time—at least, not as well made. Beloved by neighborhood locals and celebrities alike, Grange Hall's closing in 2004 was one of the first deeply felt tragedies of the modern cocktail era. Pedro went on to work for Audrey Saunders at Pegu Club, but the neighborhood has yet to find a new unpretentious and comfortable public house that serves a dependably good drink.

The Campbell Apartment

Tucked away above Grand Central Station was a classics-focused cocktail bar with a business casual dress code, operating in the splashy former residence of financier John W. Campbell. The high-ceilinged, two-level salon, with its long tiled bar under gigantic windows, felt like it was tailored specifically to New Yorkers, since one had to both know

that the bar was there and how to find its entrance. It opened in 1999 and closed in the summer of 2016 when its owner, Mark Grossich, was forced out during a questionable real estate dispute. It's set to reopen in a "more accessible" form sometime in 2017, under the Gerber Group.

The Beagle

They came for the cocktails; they stayed for the food. Cocktailians and foodies alike loved the Beagle, owned by Matt Piacentini and bartender Dan Greenbaum, for its perfect balance of coziness and creativity. Some of the city's most skilled bartenders worked there, including Tom Richter (see page 154), Abigail Gullo and Sarah Morrissey. It closed before its third birthday in 2013; it seemed as though its owners had outgrown the space, though they never relocated. Instead, Matt Piacentini opened the Up and Up in the West Village in 2015.

Louis 649

In 2012, the effects of Hurricane Sandy were felt all over lower Manhattan, where floods, electrical damage and prolonged lack of power forced many businesses to close. Some venues managed to survive the odds, and this elegant neighborhood darling on 9th Street was one of them. After shutting down for 12 days, they managed to operate without refrigeration for months, keeping up a good sense of humor and providing a cozy, friendly drinking experience, drawing local and industry crowds with their cocktails and jazzy atmosphere. However, in the fall of 2014, the bar closed for good. Owner Zachary Sharaga and his partners reopened it as Mace in 2015 with Greg Boehm of Cocktail Kingdom and head bartender Nico de Soto. Here's a taste of Louis 649's most popular cocktail, Sleeping Tiger, courtesy of Mr. Sharaga.

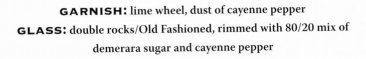

⋯ SLEEPING TIGER ⋯

GARNISH: lime wheel, dust of cayenne pepper
GLASS: double rocks/Old Fashioned, rimmed with 80/20 mix of
demerara sugar and cayenne pepper

- 1½ ounces Del Maguey Vida
- ¾ ounce lime juice
- ¼ ounce ginger syrup
- ¼ ounce honey syrup
- ½ pineapple juice

1. Shake all ingredients well with ice and double-strain into the glass over fresh ice.

2. Garnish with lime wheel perched on rim of glass and a light dusting of cayenne over the glass.

MILK & HONEY

When Sasha Petraske opened his groundbreaking Lower East Side Speakeasy on New Year's Day 2000, as bartender Tom Richter puts it, he did so with a "clean slate." His analytical approach to hospitality meant erasing everything everyone knew about cocktail service. He trained his small staff using this new perspective, formed by his meticulous mindset. It shouldn't have worked: The unmarked bar in an old Jewish tailor shop on Eldridge Street (recognizable by its TAILORS MH ALTERATIONS sign) was only accessible with possession of a number and a password (*both* of which changed on a whim), it had space for just a certain number of customers per night who had to follow strict rules of etiquette, it had no menu and it went out of its way to avoid publicity. But once all those hoops were cleared, it brought a still–unheard of level of quality to the New York City drinking experience. Petraske eventually opened Milk Honey London in April of 2002.

In a move that shocked the bar scene in late 2012, Petraske decided to close his Lower East Side location, where protégés Sam Ross and Michael McIlroy instead opened Attaboy. The bar briefly relocated to a doomed, cavernous, unfinished-yet-flashy space on East 23rd street, where it eschewed the number-and-password routine and could be easily spotted by the bouncer and line outside the door. However something called a "demolition clause" forced its closure in 2014, and despite rumors of re-opening somewhere downtown, it never did.

— Sasha Petraske —
(1973–2015)

1. No name-dropping, no star-f***ing.

2. No hooting, hollering, shouting or other loud behavior.

3. No fighting, play-fighting or talking about fighting.

4. Gentlemen will remove their hats. Hooks are provided.

5. Gentlemen will not introduce themselves to ladies. Ladies, feel free to start a conversation or ask the bartender to introduce you. If a man you don't know speaks to you, please lift your chin slightly and ignore him.

6. Do not linger outside the front door.

7. Do not bring anyone unless you would leave that person alone in your own home. You are responsible for the behavior of your guests.

8. Exit the bar briskly and silently. People are trying to sleep across the street. Please make all your travel plans and say your farewells before leaving the bar.

These were the rules of Milk Honey, the bar Sasha Petraske founded in 1999 and opened that New Year's Day on the Lower East Side. It was a splash felt around the world. On Friday, August 21, 2015, the sad news broke that he had been found dead in his home at the age of 42.

Milk Honey was one of the first CITY bars in in the modern era to offer cocktails that weren't served in a big cone-shaped Martini glass and used ingredients that were fresh and exotic—even bitter. The bar had strict rules of conduct, and everyone who worked there trained vigorously to meet meticulous levels of service detail. But by creating these rules, Petraske was breaking other ones. The world noticed, and drinking cocktails in New York was never quite the same.

So many people in the beverage industry can trace their careers directly to Petraske's influence and mentorship, and learned to pass on those traits to others (see Lucinda Sterling, page 135). After Milk Honey London opened, there came Little Branch, Dutch Kills and Middle Branch in New York, as well as the Varnish in Los Angeles and Everleigh in Melbourne, Australia.

His bars championed small, independent spirits, and he was known for being one of the guy's who *wouldn't* slam a door in the face of a new brand looking to place a product—as long as it was good. The "first time I met Sasha" stories are common in the industry, and he was known for his deep and loyal friendships.

He was also known for his cheeky sense of humor. At Milk Honey 2.0, a friend tells me Petraske overheard him tell someone on the phone that he was minutes away from leaving. Petraske turned to him and said, "There is no such thing as five minutes. There is only one last kiss, or one last drink." RIP.

You Can't Beat a Good Bar Down

Luckily, not every bar closure has a tragic ending. Here are some saloons that lived to tell more New York stories (after they'd had some work done).

Holiday Cocktail Lounge

75 St. Mark's Place
New York, NY 10003
(212) 777-9637
holidaycocktaillounge.nyc

When Holiday closed in 2012, it seemed that the East Village had died with it. Most people knew it as a grungy, dilapidated, neighborhood dive bar, with ripped vinyl seating, filthy surfaces and cheap drinks. Still, its closing hurt, and the neighborhood soon braced itself for whatever high-rent atrocity—a bank, an ugly 7/11, etc.—would open in its place.

Luckily for everyone, what ended up opening there in 2015 was . . . the Holiday Cocktail Lounge! Robert Ehrlich, founder of Pirate's Booty snack products and Barbara Sibley, owner of La Palapa restaurant next door, have given it a subtle makeover. With the guidance of Michael Neff, who is known for opening celebrated neighborhood bars like Ward3, the Rum House, Church Bar and Three Clubs (in LA) and his brother Danny Neff, an experienced bartender in his own right, they bestowed upon Holiday 2.0 just the right tone: simple, quality drinks (priced for the budget-conscious), a well chosen back bar, Long Island Iced Tea on draft and a decent beer selection (since 2016, the reins have passed to beverage manager Erik Trickett). The interior was given a good polish, unearthing a 1920s-era mural (referred to by the staff as "Zelda") after they moved the carousel-shaped bar to the center of the room.

The bar manages to put the "cocktail" back in Cocktail Lounge without coming across too stuffy, and it's become not

75 ST MARKS
HOLIDAY
COCKTAIL LOUNGE

HOLIDAY
COCKTAIL LOUNGE

From what is known as the Mixtape Menu comes this tasty drink.

GARNISH: lime twist, possibly a toy

GLASS: rocks/Old Fashioned

- 1½ ounces Damoiseau Rhum Agricole 110
- ½ ounce Amero
- ¾ ounce simple syrup ¾ ounces
- 1 ounce lime juice

Shake all ingredients with ice. Strain over fresh ice into the glass. Garnish.

only a thriving East Village destination but a service industry hang as well—prone to late night singalongs of Toto's "Africa," among other shenanigans. It's far too easy to lose all track of time of time there. "What happened to you last night?" "Aw man, I got severely Holidayed."

Dante

79-81 Macdougal Street
New York, NY 10012
(212) 982-5275
dante-nyc.com

When the charming, 100-year-old Italian West Village café closed in 2015, people were grief-stricken to lose one of its last poet cafés. Nobody expected that its reincarnation under the Australian restaurant group AvroKo would be something New York didn't know it needed: an upscale Italian restaurant with a classics-focused cocktail menu. Complete with its own Negroni section and vermouth service, Dante's new format lends the once-stodgy digs a bright, old-world European vibe. Overseen by Naren Young

(formerly of Saxon + Parole, PUBLIC and the Daily) it's one of the few venues of its kind that's open all day—including breakfast. Sipping a Garibaldi here on a warm summer's afternoon is the closest thing to a Roman Holiday that the city has to offer.

Chumley's

86 Bedford Street
New York, NY 10014
(212) 675-2081
chumleysnewyork.com

On a winding street in the West Village, with no signage apart from the number 86, lies Chumley's. Though the building dates back into the mid-19th century, it wasn't opened as a tavern until Leland Chumley bought it in 1922 to use as a speakeasy. It's the ideal building for it—a partial stable house with a back entrance off its courtyard and secret passageways built in, making it easy to flee the feds. In a barspeak, to be kicked out or to run out of something is to be "86ed," and it is almost certain that term originated here. Over the years, the

··· GARIBALDI ···

GARNISH: orange wedge, small plate or saucer
GLASS: Collins or slim highball

- 1½ ounces Campari
- fresh orange juice

1. Add 2 ice cubes to glass. Add Campari and top with a little of the juice (it will start to fluff up in the glass as it reacts to the alcohol). Stir well to combine.

2. Add one more ice cube and fill glass with more juice. Serve the glass on a saucer to catch the spill-over.

bar became a popular literary hangout, and it's where F. Scott Fitzgerald is thought to have penned parts of *The Great Gatsby*. In its sawdust-covered, pub-like heyday it attracted other notables such as Willa Cather, William Faulkner, Edna St. Vincent Millay, John Steinbeck, Ernest Hemingway, Jack Kerouac, William S. Burroughs and Dylan Thomas, among many others. By the 1970s and '80s, dust jackets of their works became a signature display, and it had one of the best, dependably outdated jukeboxes in town.

In 2007, a chimney collapse caused extensive structural damage with subsequent building code nightmares. For years, the rumors of its reopening proved to be nothing but alternative facts.

Then in 2016 restaurateur Alessandro Borgognone of Sushi Nakazawa finally reopened the space as a swank restaurant with a cocktail-focused menu. The dust jackets survived the turmoil and share wall space with portraits of its famous regulars. The sawdust floor is gone, and the only writer who can afford to eat and drink there now is J.K. Rowling, but it did clean up pretty nice—even if it's more Chumleyland than Chumley's these days.

The Long Island Bar

110 Atlantic Avenue
Brooklyn, NY 11201
(718) 625-8908
thelongislandbar.com

The big neon sign over the shuttered Long Island Restaurant on the corner of Henry and Atlantic had been dim since 2008, and everyone was clamoring to take the space over. But Emma Sullivan (of the neighborhood Montero family) and her cousins Pepita and Maruja were in no rush to lease the space. It's a long story, but somehow Toby Cecchini, who had been searching for a new place since losing his lease on Passerby, met another Montero family member by chance and was able to charm his way into an inspection with his busi-

ness partner Joel Tompkins. "He's no bahtendah," was Emma's first reaction. "Oh yeah? Feel my back, see how messed up my knees are," said Toby. At the end of the meeting she said, "He's OK." The rest is history.

The space took one and a half years to renovate. It's a myth that a clause of the lease mandated Cecchini replicate the space almost exactly as it was; rather, he preferred its 1950s charm—in fact it was more expensive to match the vintage fixtures than start fresh. When local residents voiced disapproval as they witnessed the iconic neon sign dismantled, they had no idea it was being sent for restoration at Let There Be Neon in Tribeca, (who also crafted the famous NO DANCING sign hanging between the restrooms). Funny story: a year into the bar's tenure, a group of neighborhood teens held a flash mob just in front of the sign, dancing for thirty seconds before running out the side door.

The Long Island Bar sets a comfortable neighborhood saloon atmosphere. It keeps a small, simple menu of elevated (yet affordable) variations on diner food, to go with wine, beer and cocktails. The talented roster of bartenders includes Cecchini himself, Tim Miner, Phil Ward, Jesse Harris and David Moo, who are always happy to mix off-menu on request—even a Cecchini Cosmopolitan, if you ask nicely (see page 26). The Gimlet, made with Cecchini's homemade ginger lime cordial, is an enduring customer favorite.

—Toby Cecchini's Ginger Lime Cordial—

Lime cordial, if made correctly, will keep for months or even years in the refrigerator.

- 18 limes (room temperature, very ripe, well puffed and heavy)
- 3 cups sugar
- 1 pound fresh ginger (optional)

1. Wash limes in a sinkful of warm water, scrubbing with your hands or a vegetable brush, and let them dry them on a dish towel.

2. Peel limes with a vegetable peeler, removing as little of the underlying white pith as possible. To begin each, it's helpful to cut the polar ends off, where the stem attaches and opposite. This should produce about 140 grams of peels.

3. In a non-reactive, coverable container, add sugar to the peels and stir a bit to initiate oil extraction. Make certain the peels are well covered with sugar and then leave for 8–12 hours. This makes an *oleo saccharum*—a slurry which extracts the citrus oil from the peel, incorporating it into the sugar. Set the peeled limes aside in a refrigerator.

4. The next day, cut your limes in half and juice them. This should produce about 2½ cups of juice. If you're making a ginger version, wash the ginger, peel it and cut it into smallish pieces (1" or less).

5. Combine the juice and ginger in a blender and pulse well to make a slurry that can allow the ginger to open up. Add this to the *oleo saccharum* of peels and sugar, and stir well for several minutes to entirely incorporate the juice mixture and dissolve any remaining sugar.

6. If you're not employing ginger, add the juice directly to the *oleo saccharum* and mix in the same manner.

7. Cover and refrigerate for at least 12 hours, and up to 48. When ready, strain the cordial off from the peels in a fine mesh strainer or chinoise.

8. Funnel cordial into a clean, sterile covered container or cappable bottle and return to refrigerator for another day to cure before using. Makes roughly 1 liter.

··· GIN GIMLET ···

GLASS: coupe

GARNISH: 2 thin lime wheels

- 2 ounces dry gin
- 1 ounce Ginger Lime Cordial
  (recipe on page 259)

- ¾ ounce fresh lime juice

Shake all ingredients with ice. Strain into a coupe glass. Garnish.

BESTIES

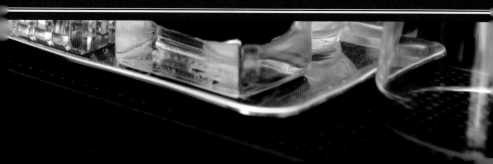

W hen I set out to write this, I was tasked with writing a "best of" chapter. It made me uncomfortable. That's because when it comes to bars and the cocktail industry, I don't like to play favorites. My favorite drink or bar is whichever one happens to be delighting my senses or providing sanctuary at any given time. I might have had an outstanding drink last night at one of my locals— but I also might have tried something new somewhere I'd never been before. Which one is best? I decided to focus on which characteristics of my drinking experience have really stood out over the years. Here are some of the best . . .let's call them "drink situations" . . .around town.

"I LOOK OUT THE WINDOW AND I SEE THE LIGHTS AND
THE SKYLINE AND THE PEOPLE ON THE STREET
RUSHING AROUND LOOKING FOR ACTION, LOVE, AND THE
WORLD'S GREATEST CHOCOLATE CHIP COOKIE, AND MY
HEART DOES A LITTLE DANCE."

*— excerpt from Heartburn
by Nora Ephron*

—Best Flavor Fakeout—

DORIAN GRAY; ANALOGUE (SEE PAGE 201 FOR BAR INFO)

"The character Dorian Gray is not all that he seems. When we made the drink, it seemed like it was going to be overly sweet and citrusy. But when we finished the creation, it was very well balanced and drier than expected. We wanted to connect it to a story where the character was not all that they seemed to be. The Scotch, dry vermouth and nutmeg bring out an unexpected profile that balances with the pear and rosemary syrup."—Analogue head bartender Zack Berger

GARNISH: freshly grated nutmeg

GLASS: coupe

- 1½ ounces Black Bottle Scotch
- ¾ ounce Pur Pear Liqueur
- ¾ ounce fresh lemon juice
- ½ ounce dry vermouth
- ½ ounce rosemary-maple syrup
- 2 dashes angostura bitters

In a cocktail shaker filled with ice, add all liquid ingredients and shake until chilled. Strain into a coupe and garnish with freshly grated nutmeg.

—*Best Balance of Floral Notes*—
GINS 'N ROSES; THE WREN

344 Bowery
New York, NY
(212) 388-0148
thewrennyc.com

"I'm constantly challenging myself to use ingredients that I find difficult to work with. In this case, rose. I had never enjoyed rosewater, but after tasting Giffard Black Rose Liqueur, I was inspired to create a cocktail that could celebrate the rose but not be dominated by it. Martin Miller Gin has a softness to it while still staying true to the London Dry style, so I often turn to it when making cocktails. Cocchi Americano Rosa is a wonderful aperitif wine that is both aromatic and slightly bitter from the quinine. These three ingredients, combined with a splash of freshly squeezed lemon juice, create a well balanced, refreshingly floral cocktail."—co-owner *Krissy Harris*

··· GINS 'N ROSES ···

GARNISH: dried rosebuds (can be purchased at health and specialty food stores)

GLASS: rocks/Old Fashioned

- 1 ounce Martin Miller's Gin
- 1 ounce Cocchi Americano Rosa
- ½ ounce fresh lemon juice
- ½ ounce Giffard Black Rose Liqueur
- ¼ ounce honey syrup (1:3 honey to water)

1. Add all the ingredients to a shaker and fill with ice.

2. Shake, and strain into an Old Fashioned glass filled with fresh ice. Garnish with dried rosebuds.

—*Best Way To Ease Into the Weekend*—
IPA OVER ICE; WILFIE & NELL

228 West 4th Street
New York, NY 10014
wilfieandnell.com

"The idea was to create a brunch drink that was not overly boozy. It's served over ice, and IPA is slightly bitter, so it's not really poundable; it's for sipping. Some people actually see it as a cure. You can have a few and not be hammered. It's not as harsh as a Bloody Mary—a Bloody Mary comes to you spicy and boozy. But the IPA Over Ice takes you a little longer to drink. If you're feeling a little fragile, it's a softer alternative to a Bloody Mary. Hopefully, after two them, you'll be feeling better."—*Simon Gibson*

··· IPA OVER ICE ···

GARNISH: orange wedge

GLASS: pint

- • 3 ounces grapefruit juice
- • 1 ounce Campari
- • dash of simple syrup
- • 8 ounces IPA

1. Combine all of the ingredients, except for the beer, in a cocktail tin and shake.

2. Strain into a pint glass filled with ice, and top with the beer. Garnish with orange wedge.

—Prettiest Non-Tomato-Based Bloody Mary—
BEET BLOODY MARY; THE PENROSE

1590 Second Avenue
New York, NY 10028
penrosebar.com

"This is a far-flung riff on a Bloody Mary cocktail I was inspired to make for a brunch with my tastes. I understand the place of savory cocktails like the traditional Bloody Mary, but I'm never able to drink a whole one—two sips and I'm done. However, I've always been envious of people who benefit from its restorative properties. First, it's probably got vitamins. Second, it's big, so you're kind of hydrating yourself (but who's kidding who here?). Third, it's got booze, so you're hair-of-the-dogging your hangover. Fourth, and perhaps most underrated of all, it's spicy: You're shocking your adrenal glands and maybe even your lymphatic system while you sit and eat Eggs Benedict. It's like exercising without doing anything . . . it performs all the necessary tasks you ask of a Bloody Mary without being gross."—*Pete Vasconcellos*

··· BEET BLOODY MARY ···

GARNISH: dried apple ring
GLASS: pint

- 2 ounces chili-infused Vodka (instructions follow)
- 1½ ounces beet juice
- 1½ ounces pressed apple juice
- ½ ounce lemon juice
- ½ ounce fresh pressed ginger juice, with equal part sugar added
- ¼ ounce orange juice
- pinch of salt

Add all the ingredients to a shaker and fill with ice. Shake, and strain into a pint glass filled with fresh ice. Garnish with a dried apple ring.

Chili-Infused Vodka

- 1 liter of vodka
- 3 jalapeños, sliced and de-seeded
- 5 dried chipotle peppers, de-seeded

Pour full contents of vodka bottle and chilies into an airtight container. Shake and let sit for 24 hours to infuse. Strain.

··· PURPLE RAIN ···

This was originally served at Amor y Amargo for Double Buzz.

GARNISH: grapefruit twist
GLASS: double rocks/Old Fashioned

- 1 ounce Zucca or Amaro Sfmuato
- 1 ounce Cocchi Rosa
- 2 dashes lavender bitters (such as Scrappy's)
- 4 ounces iced coffee (made with a medium or light roast, naturally processed African Coffee)

1. Add all ingredients in a mixing glass and give it a quick stir. The coffee will provide most of the dilution, this is just to chill the drink.

2. Pour in a tall glass and garnish with an expressed twist of grapefruit peel.

—Best Pick-Me-Up—
PURPLE RAIN AND
ESPRESSO OLD FASHIONED (NON-ALCOHOLIC)

Of course, coffee cocktails from Amanda Whitt! (Psst! Amanda really knows her coffee.)

This was originally served at Everyman Espresso, a collaboration between myself and Sam Lewontin. This is more of a modular recipe, as we served it with many espressos, exchanging bitters to compliment the different espressos. It doesn't re-invent the wheel, just applies what we love about Fashioneds to espresso—that they are a great entry point for one to appreciate something they find too strong to dive right into."—Amanda Whitt

GARNISH: orange twist

GLASS: double rocks/Old Fashioned

- 1 double shot of single-origin espresso, rested

- 2–3 dashes of bitters of your choice (look for flavors that are consistent with those found in the espresso)
- ¼ ounce rich simple syrup

Add all ingredients to mixing glass and stir until chilled. Serve in a double-rocks glass with a good piece of ice and a citrus twist.

—Best Message—
Francine Cohen

There are so many disparate working parts of the New York City cocktail community. Though she doesn't work behind a bar, writer Francine Cohen is the great unifier—bartenders, chefs, consultants, publicity teams, spirits brands, media and the rest. She has a knack for knowing exactly what to say to help them all communicate and learn from one another. As the founder of the Inside F and B website, Cohen not only covers all the top industry stories but brings a valuable maturity to the cocktail playground, with a focus on hospitality. She knows practically everyone, and if her name is attached to a project, people are happy to be involved.

"We think we're the center of the universe," she says of the city's cocktail industry. "At least we are the impetus for so much of the cocktail culture in every major city . . .When cocktails rose up on the coasts, it gave guests something new to try and it gave related businesses—farmers, distillers, winemakers, etc.—a place to raise their profile. This in turn helped bartenders get the tools and assets they needed to explore their passion."

Social media has played a key role in raising the community's profile. "Bartenders have always been popular, but now because it's easier to get the word out, they are community leaders in a way celebrity chefs have always been. [In New York City,] they've worked long and hard to make a viable, respectable career. They are artisans, and hosts—they bring a layer of legitimacy to brands and help make spirits categories grow. The town is better for them."

Cohen is particularly inspired when she sees influence of cocktail culture in the culinary world. "Bartenders have opportunities to enhance beverage programs. Seeing thoughtful cocktail menus in the finest restaurants around the world says 'we've done it.' "

—Best Place to Celebrate the City's Cultural Diversity—

THE BONNIE

29-12 23rd Avenue
Astoria, NY 11105
(718) 274-2105
thebonnie.com

"I have an infatuation with the idea of combining mezcal, pisco and cachaça. I was turned on to all three of these liquors at the same time, and I love regional spirits. Mezcal comes from Oaxaca [Mexico], Pisco comes from the Andes Mountains and Cachaça comes from Brazil. The drink also incorporates mole from Mexico, black cardamom from India and falernum from the Caribbean. New York is a city of immigrants, and its diversity is what makes our cocktail culture so rich."
—*Mike Di Tota*

GARNISH: crushed cinnamon sticks
GLASS: rocks/Old Fashioned

- ¾ ounce Buen Bicho Mezcal Joven
- ½ ounce Yaguara Cachaça
- ½ ounce toasted black cardamom and cinnamon maple syrup (instructions follow)
- ½ ounce fresh lime juice
- ¼ ounce Macchu Pisco
- ¼ ounce Rothman Winter Orchard Apricot Liqueur
- ¼ ounce Ancho Reyes Chile Liqueur
- ½ ounce orgeat
- ¼ ounce Velvet Falernum Liqueur
- 2 dashes mole bitters
- Pinch of salt

Add all ingredients to a shaker and fill with ice. Shake and strain into an Old Fashioned glass filled with crushed ice. Garnish with crushed cinnamon sticks.

Toasted Black Cardamom and Cinnamon Maple Syrup

- 1 cup maple syrup
- ½ cup water
- 2 cinnamon sticks, smashed
- 3 black cardamom pods, smashed

1. Toast the cinnamon sticks over medium heat until they release their aroma and begin to crackle.

2. Combine water and maple syrup in a small saucepan over medium heat. Add spices and simmer for five minutes. Remove from heat and let cool to room temperature.

3. Once completely cool (after about an hour), strain and discard solids. Refrigerate for up to one month.

—*Best Drink for Channeling*—
Your Inner Science Nerd
GLASGOW MILK PUNCH;
THE GANDER

15 West 18th Street
New York, NY 10011
(212) 229-9500
thegandernyc.com

"This clarified punch is served through a stout beer faucet at The Gander under a Nitrogen/CO2 blend to give it a beautifully creamy head, which dissipates to reveal the clear punch. While this can certainly be done at home with the right equipment, it can also be kept in the refrigerator and shaken over ice to deliver a nice frothiness."—*Brian Matthys*, creator

··· GLASGOW MILK PUNCH ···

GARNISH: lemon twist
GLASS: rocks/Old Fashioned

- 1½ ounces Compass Box Great King Street Glasgow Blend
- ½ ounce Compass Box Orangerie
- ½ ounce oleo saccharum (see page 92)
- 2¼ ounces whey (clarified milk with lemon)

Shake ingredients over ice, strain into a dessert wine, cocktail or rocks glass over a couple of ice cubes and garnish with a lemon twist.

> NOTE: the sweetness from the oleo saccharum may need to be lowered a bit depending on the whey's acidity level. To find your sweet spot, start with a bit less than ½ ounce and add more if needed.

—Best Down-to-Earth, Super-High-End Restaurant-Bar—

DANIEL

60 East 65th Street
New York, NY 10065
(212) 288-0033
danielnyc.com

Daniel, one of the most sophisticated restaurants in the entire city, happens to house a surprisingly approachable and comfortable bar alcove. Marcie Anderson created this fetching cocktail to marry two national spirits: cachaça from Brazil with shochu from Japan.

··· LOST IN TRANSLATION ···

GARNISH: dusting of matcha powder

GLASS: clay bowl

- 1 ounce Avuá Prata Cachaça
- 1 ounce Mizu Shochu
- ½ ounce fresh lime juice
- ¾ ounce simple syrup
- ¼ teaspoon Wakatake Matcha Powder (from In Pursuit Of Tea)
- ¾ ounce egg white

1. Dry shake for 10 seconds, then shake with ice.

2. Double strain into clay bowl. Top with a light dusting of matcha powder.

—*Best Cosmopolitan Update*—
FLOWER, ROKC

3452 Broadway
New York, NY 10031
rockynyc.com

This ramen restaurant in Harlem makes some of the most innovative cocktails in the city right now. The Flower is a a customer favorite, which infuses a traditional Cosmopolitan with floral accents without making you feel as though you're drinking potpourri.

··· FLOWER ···

GARNISH: lavender sprig

GLASS: the restaurants serves this in a bulb glass,
but you can use a coupe or Martini glass

- 1 ounce Mizu 'Saga Barley' Shochu infused with lavender
- ½ ounce St-Germain liqueur
- 2 ounce cranberry juice cocktail
- ¼ ounce lime juice

1. Infuse a few dried lavender blossoms (available at health food and specialty food stores) into the shochu, ideally for 1–2 days prior to use in cocktail.

2. Add all ingredients to shaker, shake with ice and strain.

··· ÉMILE ZOLA (J'ACCUSE) ···

GARNISH: basil leaf

GLASS: coupe

- 1½ ounces grappa Candolini
- ¾ ounce Calvados
- ½ ounce vermouth blanc
- 4 dashes blackstrap bitters

Stir all ingredients with ice. Strain into the coupe. Garnish with the leaf rested over the drink in the glass.

—Best Cocktail Named for a Multinational Naturalist—
ÉMILE ZOLA; AUGUST LAURA

August Laura
387 Court Street
Brooklyn, NY 11231

Death & Co veterans Alyssa Sartor and Frankie Rodriguez opened this Carroll Gardens bar as an homage to Sartor's grandfather, who grew up in the neighborhood when it was primarily Italian. The focus here is on Italian ingredients, especially inventive uses of spirits like grappa, amaro and other less celebrated liqueurs like nocino and amaretto. This cocktail combines grappa and Calvados. It was originally served to my friend John Hedigan as a bartender's choice experiment; since I have a deep superstition about drinking unnamed cocktails anywhere around me, John decided on this name, as Zola was a French writer with an Italian heritage.

··· AMARETTO SOUR ···

GARNISH: grated nutmeg

GLASS: coupe

- 1½ ounces Gozio Amaretto
- ½ ounce Don Ciccio Nocino
- 1 ounce lemon juice, freshly squeezed
- ¼ ounce simple syrup
- egg white

1. Add all ingredients to a shaker. Dry shake for 15 seconds.

2. Add ice and shake again for at least 20 seconds. Strain into the coupe and grate nutmeg over the top.

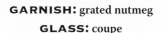

—Best Amaretto Sour—

AUGUST LAURA

One of the only cocktails on the menu I refused to order at August Laura was the Amaretto Sour, until I saw one served to another patron. Its cumulus froth seduced me like a peacock in heat, and then I noticed that Sartor's recipe includes a really high quality amaretto and adds a touch of earthy nocino to elevate it from the cloying '70s swill we all think of.

··· GREYFRIAR ···

GARNISH: orange twist

GLASS: coupe

- ½ ounce Campari
- ½ ounce Fino sherry
- ½ ounce sweet vermouth
- 1 ounce blended Scotch
- ½ ounce peated Scotch

Stir all ingredients with ice. Strain into coupe. Garnish.

—Best Newcomer Bar—

PIG BLEECKER

155 Blecker Street
New York, NY 10012
(646) 756-5115

Cocktails are typically an afterthought at most barbecue restaurants. But as barbecue cuisine becomes more serious in the city, so do the cocktails. Here's one from beverage director Sarah Morrissey, formerly of Dear Irving and the Beagle.

GARNISH: cherry

GLASS: coupe

- 1½ ounces Bourbon
- 1 ounce Oloroso sherry
- ½ ounce Cherry Heering
- ½ ounce Black Strap Rum (Cruzan)
- ¼ ounce Cynar
- Barspoon Nocino (Teoh uses Nux Alpina)
- 1 Dash Bittermens Burlesque Bitters

Stir all ingredients with ice. Strain into a coupe glass. Garnish.

FROM BRYAN: A Dash of a dry orange bitters such as Regan's could work if Bittermens is not available. I would not suggest using Fee Brothers.

—Best Drink for When New York Is Bringing You Down—
THE THIN VEIL

"This was made for a now-defunct band of a friend called Tin Veil. Like the music of its namesake, this cocktail is big and will knock you on your butt if you're not careful. It has a sort of esoteric appeal for those with a taste for something on the dark side."*—Bryan Teoh*

—*Best Vermouth Showcase*—
VERMOUTH COBBLER; LaRINA PASTIFICIO E VINO

387 Myrtle Avenue
Brooklyn, NY 11205
(718) 852-0001
larinabk.com

Owned by Giulia Peliccioni, Robert Aita and chef Silvia Barban, this Italian restaurant in Fort Greene is a great place to enjoy a vermouth lesson (not to mention an impeccable meal). This easy, low-ABV cocktail is perfect for some light, refreshing sipping.

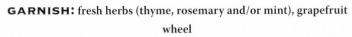

GARNISH: fresh herbs (thyme, rosemary and/or mint), grapefruit
wheel
GLASS: rocks/Old Fashioned

- 2 ounces Imbue Bittersweet
  Vermouth
- 1 ounce Silvio Carta Vermouth
- ½ ounce lemon juice

Build the drink in the glass and stir with plenty of ice. Garnish.

—Best Dirty Martini Alternative—
McClure's Pickle Martini; Bua

122 Saint Mark's Place
New York, NY 10009
(212) 979-6276
buabar.com

"I think I came up with the drink late at night at Bua in the early days, with our regular and good friend PJ Calapa. We served McClure's Pickles from the beginning, as a side dish for sliders and grilled cheese sandwiches. It seemed a good way to use the brine while creating a savory cocktail, so we started to make them initially as an alternative to dirty Martinis for people we knew liked pickles. Eventually the drink went on the menu and has become a staple for us."—*Simon Gibson*

GARNISH: pickle slice

GLASS: Martini or coupe

- 2 ounces vodka or gin
- 1 ounce McClure's Pickle juice

Add all the ingredients to a mixing glass and fill with ice. Stir until very cold and strain into a chilled cocktail glass. Garnish with pickle slice.

—Best Place to Drink Still to Glass—
THE SHANTY AT NY DISTILLING CO.

79 Richardson Street
Brooklyn, NY 11222
(718) 878-3579
nydistilling.com/theshanty

The Big Iron is a signature cocktail from the Shanty, the bar at NY Distilling Co. (see page 334) that features a window onto the main distillery floor, where the spirits themselves are made:

GARNISH: broad orange and lemon twists
GLASS: rocks/Old Fashioned

- 2 ounces Mister Katz's Rock Rye
- 1 dash Angostura Bitters
- 1 dash orange Bitters

Stir ingredients over ice and strain into glass filled with ice. Garnish with broad orange and lemon twists.

··· THE MNTOWER ···

GARNISH: lime (expressed and discarded)

GLASS: coupe

- 2 ounces Plantation Stiggins' Fancy Pineapple Rum
- 1½ ounces Wölffer Estate Verjus
- ¼ ounce Smith Cross rum
- ¼ ounce pineapple syrup (recipe follows)

Add all ingredients into a mixing glass with ice and stir. Strain into the glass. Express lime twist over top and discard.

Pineapple Syrup

- 1 pineapple, cut into 1-inch cubes
- 1 quart of sugar

Combine in large cambro (storage container) for 4 hours. Blend and strain out the juices with chinois.

—Best Juiceless Daiquiri—

THE MOONTOWER, ATTRIBUTED TO JESSE HARRIS

Think of this as a stirred pineapple Daiquiri. It offers the brightness of a shaken drink while staying spirit-forward and having a mouth feel similar to a Martini."—*Jesse Harris*

GARNISH: lemon twist

GLASS: double rocks/Old Fashioned

- 1 ounce El Dorado 12-Year Rum
- 1 ounce Santa Teresa 1796 Rum
- ½ ounce Amaro Sibilia
- ½ ounce Giffard Banane de Bresil
- 2 dashes Bittermens Tiki Bitters

1. Combine all ingredients in a mixing glass. Add ice and stir to chill and dilute.

2. Strain into a chilled double Old Fashioned glass with one large ice cube. Garnish with a lemon twist.

—Best Stirred Tiki Drink—

THE MONKEY'S UNCLE, BY TIM MINER

"Hey, Tim. I want a tiki cocktail but I want it stirred. Oh, and think you can use some of that delicious Giffard Banane de Brasil and Amaro Sibilia? Thanks!" —Amanda Schuster during one long evening at Long Island Bar

—Best Boozy Shutterbug—
Gabi Porter

I'm one of those people who hates having their picture ta[ken]
when I'm attending an industry event and professional fo[od-and-]
drink photographer Gabi Porter is behind the camera, I jus[t]
let her do her thing. She has a way of capturing the perfec[t]
moment and expression, and always makes her subjects fe[el like a]
star. I hear her say, "Oh!" and grin and I know it's going to [be a great]
shot. Her tabletop photos come out beautifully too. How d[oes she]
always seem to know our best side? Or sense when to sna[p a per-]
fect 3 A.M. '80s-singalong moment at Holiday? She shares a[bout]
her background here:

ON HER INSPIRATION: "I'm a barfly. I have been since I w[as too]
young to drink. I know the rhythm and the unspoken langua[ge,]
which makes it easier to anticipate a shot that I see is abou[t]
I try not to insert my own will and ego into a photo. I think [the]

you feel when you're taking a photo is apparent in the photos you end up with, and bars are my happy place so that is quite enough ego for me. Plus so many of the people behind bars in NYC are my good friends, and photos become a conversation, not a monologue."

ON ONE OF HER FAVORITE BAR PHOTOS: "I once shot the opening of 21 Greenpoint, the restaurant and bar owned by Homer Murray, and Bill Murray (Homer's dad) was bartending the opening. I had been running around taking pictures for a couple of hours and finally decided I needed a drink. So I edged my way up to the bar and found myself standing next to this woman who was screaming, 'Do you have a nice Barolo?' at Bill on repeat. She was trying to be funny and not succeeding. Everyone was shrinking away from her and Bill sort of glanced at her, and then right past her, and his eyes landed on me standing there, and he gives me the bartender chin jerk. That chin jerk says everything. It says, 'You're next.' It says, 'What do you want?' I signal back, 'A shot of tequila.' And he furrows his brow and looks me up and down and makes a square sign with his fingers. I got carded by Bill Murray. And we did the whole thing without saying a word."

··· ABERDEEN ···

GARNISH: orange peel
GLASS: rocks/Old Fashioned

- 2 ounces Black Bottle Scotch
- ½ ounce Lapsang Souchong tea syrup (add two bags of the tea to 1:1 simple syrup recipe, strain and allow to cool)
- 2 dashes Jack Rudy Aromatic Bitters

Build the drink in the glass and stir with ice. Express the peel over the drink and place in the glass.

—Best Scottish Journey By Way of Brooklyn—
ABERDEEN; TRAVEL BAR

520 Court Street
Brooklyn, NY 11231
(718) 858-2509
travelbarbrooklyn.com

It's fitting that the drinks served at this Carroll Gardens bar (owned by Mike Vacheresse) always feel so transportive. His cocktail combines slightly smoky blended Scotch with tea syrup, projecting a feeling of settling in by a fireplace in the Scottish Highlands.

··· THE DITMARS 35-01 ···

GARNISH: orangle wheel

GLASS: coupe

- 1½ ounces Queens Courage Old Tom-Style gin
- ¾ ounce Licor Beirão
- ½ ounce fresh lime juice
- 2 barspoons Fernet Branca

1. Add all ingredients to a cocktail shaker filled with ice. Gently roll the shaker (so as to avoid bruising the gin) until chilled.

2. Strain into a coupe and float ½ an orange wheel on top as garnish.

—*Best Portuguese Journey By Way of Queens*—
THE DITMARS 35-01 BY TARCISIO COSTA

This cocktail pairs Licor Beirão, a native of Portugal, and Queens Courage gin made in Astoria.

··· SEITHENNIN (LOST TO THE SEA) ···

GARNISH: pickled rack seaweed
GLASS: Martini

- 2 ounces Sipsmith VJOP gin
- ½ ounce Chartreuse
- kelp bitters
- laver oil

1. Stir gin and Chartreuse with ice until chilled.

2. Rim Martini glass with powdered laver seaweed. Add a splash of kelp bitters.

3. Strain gin and chartreuse into martini glass. Add pickled wrack seaweed as garnish. Finish with a few drops of laver oil.

—Best Welsh Journey By Way of Brooklyn—

SEITHENNIN; SUNKEN HUNDRED

276 Smith Street
Brooklyn, NY 11231
(718) 722-1069
sunkenhundred.nyc

Named for a sunken, petrified forest off the coast of Wales, this Welsh restaurant in Carroll Gardens is known for its seaweed-focused cuisine (you have not lived till you've eaten their homemade seaweed cheese puffs). When brothers Illtyd and Dominic Barrett opened the place in 2016, they wanted a signature drink to match the theme. This cocktail's kelp bitters and laver oil are made in-house. It sounds (and looks) crazy, but it works.

—Best MacGyver-esque Mixer—
MIKEY DIEHL; DREXLER'S

Drexler's
9 Avenue A
New York, NY 10009
(646) 524-5226
drexlersnyc.com

One trait possessed by any great bartender is an ability to ad-lib when necessary. Here Mikey Diehl of Drexler's shares a variation on a classic cocktail, conjured up when circumstances demanded a little improvisation.

"Before I ever relied on the cocktail industry to pay my rent, I was just a clueless fancy cocktail fanatic. I would go into any bar where the vibe was fitting to ask for a cocktail, instead of just a gin and tonic or some crap on tap. The problem was that I really didn't know any cocktails by name, so I followed a blind impulse—'Umm, can you make a Sidecar?' It would usually throw the bartender for a loop, as they had not made one since bartending school. Some came with lemon twists, some came with orange juice, some came with bourbon; I was too green to know the difference, let alone call someone out on any mistakes. It became my first regular drink. I had good ones, bad ones, small ones, big ones. When I started working with Vince [Favella] down at Ward3, we nailed down my favorite way to serve it: short-pour the sugar-rimmed cocktail glass (so it doesn't spill over and get everything sticky), and serve the extra in a shot glass! A SIDECAR FOR YOUR SIDECAR!"—*Mikey Diehl*

··· HAWAIIAN WAR CHANT ···

In the "middle of my time at Ward3 I fell hard for tiki cocktails and culture, but the crowd being as whiskey-driven as they were down there, Daiquiris were always a hard pitch. So I struggled to come up with a boozy and stirred tiki-style cocktail. All research led me to two of my recurring trends in classic recipes: grapefruit + cinnamon, and Angostura + absinthe. It turned out to be a hit. I think that it's slightly out of place in a whiskey bar, but still fits the tone. Maybe that's a little reflective of myself?"—*Mikey Diehl*

GARNISH: orange twist
GLASS: rocks/Old Fashioned

- **2 ounces quality aged rum (my favorite is Plantation Original Dark)**
- **¼ ounce grapefruit liqueur (Giffard's is top notch)**
- **¼ ounce cinnamon syrup**
- **1 dash Angostura Bitters**
- **1 dash Absinthe**

Stir with ice until well chilled. Strain and serve over fresh ice with an orange twist.

Best of the Rest

Best bar snacks: chicken wings at Bar Goto; spicy shrimp arepas at Leyenda; oysters at Grand Army with medicine dropper sauces

Best bar sandwich: turkey leg confit at Henry Public (329 Henry Street, Brooklyn)

Best bar entrée: anything at Cherry Point; burger at Slowly Shirley; Mofongo at Leyenda

Best brunch: Leyenda; Clover Club (bacon tasting menu!); Mother's Ruin; Irish breakfast at Dead Rabbit

Most welcoming: Dead Rabbit and BlackTail, which offer a complimentary cup of punch and a mini Daiquiri, respectively, upon seating

Best bar to visit alone to make friends (or at least influence people): Amor y Amargo

Best bar to visit if you want to be alone unless ordering a drink: Raines Law Room

Best place for an aperitif: Dear Irving; Caffe Dante

Best place to end the night: Holiday Cocktail Lounge

Best blameless guilty pleasure: the Grasshopper at Long Island Bar; Long Island Iced Tea on draft at Holiday Cocktail Lounge

Best hotel bars: Rum House; Langham Hotel (400 Fifth Ave)

Best bar for drinking with celebrity ghosts: '21' Club

Best bars with a classic jazzy nightclub vibe, without the terrible 2-drink minimum: Flatiron Room (37 West 26th Street, Manhattan); Fine Rare (9 East 37th Street, Manhattan)

Best bars for when you just want a fking drink:** Drexler's; Boilermaker; Long Island Bar

NEW YORK STATE OF MIND

Now that you have most of the recipes, it's time to set the mood. Here's a little music, a podcast to download, some people to meet and a way that bartending can actually save lives. It's also important to know where to capture that New York groove outside of town.

"WHEN YOU LEAVE NEW YORK,
YOU AIN'T GOING ANYWHERE."

—Jimmy Breslin

Patrons of the Arts

Of course the cocktail community would be nowhere if no one bothered visiting the bars. When cocktailing around town, chances are you'll run into these convivial married bar regulars somewhere along the way—that is, if they're not throwing a spectacular gathering at home.

Colleen Newvine Tebeau and John Tebeau

Colleen and John are the ultimate bon vivants—it seems like they know everyone! That's because these two gifted conversationalists have a way of deftly engaging people and genuinely making everyone around them feel like long lost friends, even if they've only just met. John can be found parttime behind the stick at Fort Defiance in Red Hook, and his extra bartender training has helped make the monthly Spaghetti Nights and occasional Living Room Concerts at their Brooklyn Heights apartment the stuff of legends. Here is a recipe they like to serve at home, with a bit of explanation from each of them.

··· GOOD OLD FASHIONED DAIQUIRI ···

"John started making Daiquiris with fresh lime juice in the late '90s, inspired by a recipe deck and a bowl full of limes at a friend's house. We'd never seen a bartender make one, and everyone we knew only thought of Daiquiris as those frozen resort drinks, so for years we called them 'Hemingway Daiquiris' to differentiate from the Slurpee-like version. When we moved to New York and started going to cocktail bars much later, we learned that there's an actual drink named Hemingway Daiquiri, with grapefruit juice and maraschino liqueur." —Colleen Newvine Tebeau

GARNISH: none   **GLASS:** coupe or wine glass

- 2 ounces rum
- Juice of 1 lime, freshly squeezed
- ¾ ounce simple syrup (1:1 sugar to water, fully dissolved; bonus points for hippie sugar like "Sugar in the Raw")

1. Add ingredients to a shaker full of ice cubes, and shake it till you feel frostbite in your hands.

2. Pour into a chilled, stemmed cocktail glass. (Use a wine glass in a pinch). John would put the glasses into the freezer at least 10 minutes before serving, then pull them out at the last second.

3. Drink quickly.

"When choosing the rum, use whatever you have on hand. Light, dark, amber, new, old, lousy, fancy—it doesn't matter. Use whatever rum you got. Different rums will give you different Daiquiris, and they'll all be good. Colleen's favorites are El Dorado 12-year for a rich, indulgent drink and Plantation 5-Year for a good everyday, but we've always used whatever we have on the bar." — John Tebeau

Nicole and Joe Desmond

The Desmonds are the proprietors of the Rhum Rhum Room, an invite-only tiki bar "somewhere in the West Village" that is complete with a menagerie of felines and exotic birds, including a very precocious parrot named Sheena who insists on being the center of attention. These two are always dressed to impress. It could be the dankest, soggiest, coldest, dreariest night of the year and Nicole will still step out in a proper *outfit*—dress, shoes, hair accessory, jewelry, handbag and all. Joe will match at least some component of his attire to compliment Nicole, if the two are not entirely matching. Neither of them is a professional bartender, writer or brand manager, yet they are regular supporters of many establishments. Joe and Nicole know so many people within the industry that they seem as integral to it as the bartenders themselves.

One of the perks of being invited to the Rhum Rhum Room (aside from Sheena dancing when you sing "Sheena is a Punk Rocker" to her) are Joe's punches and deep-cut tiki cocktails made from vintage. Here is their house punch recipe.

··· RHUM RHUM ROOM PUNCH ···

GARNISH: drinker's choice

GLASS: punch cup

- 16 ounces lime juice
- 16 ounces orange juice
- 16 ounces pineapple juice
- 16 ounces Alize Passionfruit liqueur with cranberry
- 8 ounces Smith Cross Rum

- 16 ounces dark Jamaican Rum (such as Myers's Original Dark)
- 8 ounces Bacardi 151 Rum
- 8 ounces simple syrup
- 8 ounces honey

Add all ingredients to a punch bowl with a block of ice and stir. Serve in punch cups.

Speed Rack

The Speed Rack female bartending competition was founded in 2011 by Ivy Mix (now co-owner of Leyenda) and Lynnette Marrero (now beverage director of the Llama Inn in Williamsburg, Brooklyn) to raise money for breast cancer awareness charities. As of press time, they've raised over $500,000 globally. This bartending race began in New York and now takes place in seven other domestic regions, in addition to several European cities, with a "Miss Speed Rack" crowned after each competition. Once each region meets separately, the victors meet each other in a final showdown.

The competition consists of several bartending heats between two women bartenders, who are evaluated not only for time but accuracy and drink presentation as well. Drinks are judged by a rotating panel of industry veterans, like Audrey Saunders, Julie Reiner, Jim Meehan of PDT, Aisha Sharpe, Dale DeGroff and David Wondrich, as well as chefs and drinks writers. Speed Rack is as much a spectator sport as it is a bartending contest, and spirits brands sponsor the events for both on stage use and audience refreshment. As you might expect, it gets wild in there! To learn more about Speed Rack, visit speed-rack.com.

Setting Up Your Home Bar

Here are some essential tools, glassware and basic items to stock before you begin mixing some recipes from the following pages.

Stocking Tips

1. Start with some decent base spirits—a dry gin, some whiskey (ideally a rye, bourbon, Irish whiskey and blended or entry-level single-malt Scotch) white rum, vodka and dark rum. From here, perhaps grape-based brandy (Cognac VSOP or other equivalent), and tequila blanco (always make sure it's 100% agave). These don't have to be expensive to be of good quality. It's worth doing some online research into brands that deliver good value for cocktail mixing, or seeking advice at the liquor store (my site alcoholprofessor.com has some suggestions). Subcategories of this booze (other aged rums, rhum agricole, aged tequila, Old Tom gin, etc.) and any other spirits not mentioned like mezcal, pisco and cachaça are also worth the investment, but this is a good place to start.

2. Invest in a few liqueurs and aperitifs. It is important to stock Campari or similar "red" aperitivos (Contratto, Aperol, Cappelletti, etc.) for anything in the Negroni family of cocktails, as they mix with almost every base spirit. For liqueurs, it's handy to keep at the very least an orange curaçao and a maraschino liqueur (found in all classic "improved" cocktail recipes), but there are many other options to consider—different fruit flavors, elderflower and ginger liqueur, to name a few.

3. Stock at least one dry (white) and one sweet (red) vermouth (fortified wine with an herbal infusion) and keep them fresh—that means unopened or refrigerated and used within a couple of months at most. Sounds snobby, but taste a fresh bottle versus one that's been absorb-

ing leftover Thai food odors in your fridge and you'll understand. Vermouth is a wonderful thing and varies considerably according to producer, style, levels of sweetness, dryness and herbaceousness (not to mention price). Martini Rossi, Dolin, Carpano Antico and Cocchi are the most popular options, but there are so many available these days that it's worth some tasting and familiarization. Ideally, you'll want to sip it neat or on the rocks, not only in mixed drinks.

4. Modern cocktail recipes call for bitter or herbal liqueurs such as amaro, fernet, chartreuse, gentian, quina, chinato, pine derivations and others. Most often these ingredients only make up a tiny fraction of a drink recipe, but they are worth keeping on hand—especially since most of them also happen to be delicious when sipped neat or with a spritz, once palates are acclimated to these seemingly exotic flavors. It's an overwhelmingly large category, and it can become quite the investment to collect them. Still, it's well worth testing them out at bars (most modern bartenders are happy to arrange flights or tastings) to decide which ones to stock at home.

5. About cocktail bitters: it's confusing, but they are not the same as bitter liqueurs. These are concentrated tinctures—recipes of herbs and other flavors—infused into high-proof alcohol and sold in small dropper bottles. For most drinks, only a couple of drops are necessary. Think of them as the integral, final seasoning to a recipe, like salt or pepper is to food. Making things more confusing, everybody and their Aunt Martha markets their artisanal flavors these days, from spicy to fruity to smoky to chocolaty to flowery. Many of them are indeed fabulous, and some bars carry entire flavor spectra of bitters. But if you're on a budget, the only bitters you really need at home, considering expense and shelf life, are Angostura (a savory mix that can be found in almost any grocery store), a good orange bitter like Regan's No. 6 and perhaps Peychaud's, another classic which differs from Angostura with its intense spice-like quality.

6. Ice: a real cocktail nerd will want to keep an array of different cubes, and (if they really want to go for it) can even invest in a separate ice freezer. Whatever your preference, the important thing is to keep the ice fresh and free of odors, which affect a drink more than you might expect. Refresh your trays every couple of days or just buy ice at a store to ensure ice neutrality (it sounds silly, I know). Optimizing ice freshness is another cocktail topic worth some additional research.

7. Garnishes:
• Make sure to use fresh citrus—lemons, limes, oranges and grapefruit at room temperature, so they're at their juiciest. The jucier the citrus, the better their oils will interact with the drinks.

• Cocktail cherries—please don't ruin a cocktail with nuclear-era hubba hubba bright pink synthetic nastiness! Use real brandied, bourboned or maraschino cherries. Recommended brands are Luxardo, Jack Rudy, Amarena, Morello and Woodford Reserve. I also highly recommend making your own when sour cherries are in season in mid summer:

- **1 pound fresh sour cherries, stems removed**
- **½ cup water**
- **½ cup sugar, any variety**
- **1–2 scrapes of fresh nutmeg**
- **¾ cup of spirit (best with bourbon, dark brandy or dark rum, or a combination)**

- **¼ cup maraschino liqueur or a mild Amaro such as Nonino, Ramazotti or Montenegro**
- **1 vanilla bean (optional)**
- **1 stick cinnamon (optional)**

1. Heat the sugar, water and cinnamon on low heat for several minutes, until sugar is dissolved and becomes a bit syrupy. Remove from heat.

2. Add the cherries and coat well with the syrup. Add the booze and vanilla (if using) and stir to coat. Let cool.

3. Carefully transfer the cherries and then the boozy syrup to the glass jar, turn it over a couple of times for good measure and then store in refrigerator. Ideally, let them steep at least overnight before use. These will last several months to a year—if you don't devour them before then.

Glassware

With the recent bell-jar-as-drinking-vessel phenomenon, this may seem like an afterthought, but glass shape really does affect the whole experience. Ideally one should have:

• Medium-sized wine glasses

• Old Fashioned (a.k.a. rocks) glasses—short and stemless

• Coupes (sometimes referred to as a Champagne glass in older recipes, or a "cocktail glass")

• Martini glasses

• Tall glasses (highballs, 10–12 ounces, and/or Collinses, 12–14 ounces) Others shapes and sizes, such as flutes and Nick & Nora (mini coupes), tiki mugs, mule tins, julep cups and blazer mugs, are less necessary but still fun. Whether you want to include them depends on your preferences and your budget.

Tools

Here's everything you may need to mix the cocktail of your dreams:

• Mixing glass—either the pint glass portion of a Boston Shaker, or a large glass with a spout (Yarai); these are used with a julep strainer (see below)

• Tin-on-tin shaker/Boston shaker—two parts that can form a tight seal. They are often sold with the mixing glass as the other half of the shaker (a.k.a. the Boston Shaker), though those run the risk of the glass shattering. Two tins that fit together or a cobbler shaker (the one with a removable cap) is the way to go

• Hawthorne strainer—used to strain from a shaker tin

• Julep strainer—perforated metal with a flat shape, used to strain from the mixing glass

• Mesh strainer—smaller and handled; used for double-straining or fine straining

• Bar spoon—long and thin with a twirled handle

• Jiggers (1 ounce/2 ounce and .5 ounce/.75 ounce)

• Citrus peeler (Y-peeler)

• Cutting board

• Sharp pairing or channel knife for cutting garnishes

• Muddler

- Microplane for spices and citrus

- Measuring spoons

- Measuring cup

- Ice bucket

- Ice scoop

- Swizzle sticks (hey, you never know)

- Matches

TECHNIQUES

Most of the cocktails in this book use the same techniques and preparations. Here's a handy reference guide, all in one place.

CHILLING GLASSWARE There are three ways to go about this:

1. Fill the glass with ice and just a little water while preparing the cocktail. Empty just before straining the drink into the glass.

2. Keep the glass refrigerated for at least an hour. Many cocktail bars have a dedicated glassware fridge for this purpose.

3. Pop the glass in the freezer as the drink is being prepared. This usually does the trick!

DRY SHAKE Shake ingredients together in a sealed shaker without ice for about 15 seconds. This is usually for drinks that require additional emulsifying, like sours and flips.

DOUBLE STRAIN Most shaken drinks only require one strain with the Hawthorne strainer. But for particularly pulpy drinks, or those containing fine seeds or tiny shards of ice, hold a fine mesh strainer level over the glass when pouring through the Hawthorne, then give it a couple of gentle taps over the glass. This ensures a smoother, creamier consistency.

EXPRESS Hold a citrus peel skin side–down over the cocktail glass and give it a quick squeeze to allow the essential oils to spritz over the finished cocktail.

SHAKE Shake specified ingredients with ice in a sealed shaker until properly chilled. This usually takes about 15 seconds—longer when there's egg or dairy involved.

SYRUP Usually this is a 1:1 recipe ("simple syrup"). Combine 1 cup granulated sugar in a saucepan with 1 cup of water. Stir over low-medium heat until dissolved. Let cool, then store in an airtight container in the refrigerator for up to a week.

- **For demerara syrup:** Replace the granulated with demerara sugar
- **For rich syrup:** Use 2 cups of sugar
- **For honey syrup:** Replace sugar in the 1:1 recipe with honey

STIR This seems self-explanatory, but it's not the same as stirring cake mix. Holding the barspoon with its back to the glass, swirl the ingredients to incorporate and chill. Condensation should form on the glass—try not to hold it while stirring, so the warmth of your hand doesn't interfere with you cooling and diluting the cocktail.

SUGARED RIM Fill a small, shallow bowl with about ¼ cup of water or citrus juice. Spread a thin layer of granulated sugar on a plate or saucer. Dip the rim of the glass first in the liquid, then in the sugar. Voilà!

- **For a salt rim:** Simply replace the sugar with salt.

Where To Purchase Ingredients and Tools in New York City

Every store listed here is unique to New York City. If you don't happen to be in town, most of these products can be found online.

Wine and Spirits

It's often said that it was easier to drink in this town during Prohibition. Today, each state has its own unique laws about where and how to purchase alcohol, and for some reason New York City has its own confusing legislation within the state. It is illegal to sell wine and hard liquor in any retail establishment that also sells food, so those items can only be sold in a liquor store. As an added headscratcher, liquor stores can't sell beer. In other words, more than one stop is often necessary. The silver lining is most of the staff you meet will really know their products and be able to help with any purchasing dilemma. Here are some liquor stores around town that are well stocked for your boozy errands.

Manhattan

Ambassador Wine and Spirits—Midtown East, 1020 Second Avenue, (212) 421-5078

Astor Wine and Spirits—East Village, 399 Lafayette Street, (212) 674-7500

Beacon Wine and Spirits—Upper West Side, 2120 Broadway, (212) 877-0028

Bottlerocket Wine and Spirits—Chelsea/Flatiron, 5 West 19th Street, (212) 929-2323

Chelsea Wine Vault—Chelsea, Chelsea Market (79 9th Avenue), (212) 462-4244

La Vid—West Village, 315 Avenue of the America's (6th Avenue), (212) 242-4545

Mister Wright Fine Wines and Spirits—Upper East Side, 1593 3rd Avenue, (212) 722-4564

Park Avenue Liquors—Midtown, 292 Madison Avenue, (212) 685-2442

Brooklyn

BQE Wine and Liquor—Williamsburg, 504 Meeker Avenue, (718) 389-3833

Best Buy Liquors—near Coney Island, 1613 Neptune Avenue, (718) 265-4350

Bibber and Bell—East Williamsburg, 418 Union Avenue, (718) 599-2000

Borisal Liquor and Wine (a.k.a. DrinkUp NY)—Park Slope, 468 4th Avenue, (800) 634-6125

Queens

36th Avenue Wine and Spirits—Long Island City, 3014 36th Ave, (718) 361-6080

Dexter Wine and Spirits—Woodhaven, 75-13 Jamaica Avenue, (718) 296-0142

Sherry Lehmann—Upper East Side, 505 Park Avenue, (212) 838-7500

Warehouse Wine and Spirits—East Village, 735 Broadway, (212) 982-7770

Gowanus Wine Merchants—Gowanus, 493 Third Avenue, (718) 499-9700

Heights Chateau—Brooklyn Heights, 123 Atlantic Avenue, (718) 330-0963

Long's Wine and Spirits—Bay Ridge, 7917 5th Avenue, (718) 748-6505

Smith and Vine—Carroll Gardens, 317 Smith Street, (718) 243-2864

Grand Wine and Liquor—Astoria, 3005 31st Street, (347) 896-8195

JC Wine and Spirits—Woodside, 39-70 61st Street, (718) 424-3546

PJ Wine—4898 Broadway, (718) 361-6080

City Wine Cellar—2295 Richmond Avenue, (718) 494-1400

Tools and Accessories

Don't worry if you miss them in the city—these shops have online stores as well.

Bowery Kitchen Supplies—Chelsea Market, 88 10th Avenue, (212) 376-4982, bowerykitchens.com

Cocktail Kingdom (also cocktail books) - 36 West 25th Street, (212) 647-9166, cocktailkingdom.com

Master Kitchen Supplies—38 Delancey Street, (212) 674-2002, masterkitchensuppliesnyc.com

Bitters, Herbs and Spices

Amor y Amargo —(also for books and tools, open after 5pm), 443 East 6th Street, Manhattan, (212) 614-6818

Dual Specialty—91 First Avenue, Manhattan, (212) 979-6045

Kalustyan's—123 Lexington Avenue, Manhattan, (800) 352-3541, kalustyans.com

The Meadow—523 Hudson Street, Manhattan, (212) 645-4633, themeadow.com

Sahadi's—187 Atlantic Avenue, Brooklyn, (718) 624-4550

Sunrise Mart—three Manhattan locations (East Village, SoHo and Midtown), (212) 598-1834

Best Local Stores For Glassware, Accessories and Entertaining Supplies

Authentiques (second hand, collectibles)— 255 West 18th Street, (212) 675-2179

Cure Thrift Store—111 East 12th Street, Manhattan, (212) 505-7467

Fishs Eddy—889 Broadway, (212) 420-9020, fishseddy.com

Pearl River Mart (best place for a cheap punch bowl!)—395 Broadway, Manhattan, (800) 878-2446, pearlriver.com

Stirling Place—363 Atlantic Avenue, Brooklyn (Park Slope) (718) 797-5667

Whisk—231 Bedford Avenue, Brooklyn (Williamsburg), (718) 218-7230

Notable Locally Made Spirits

Astoria Distilling (astoriadistilling.com): Queen's Courage Gin, an Old Tom–style gin made in Astoria, Queens

Barrow's Intense (barrowsintense.com): ginger liqueur made in Brooklyn

Breuckelen Distilling (brkdistilling.com): Glorious Gin (a cross between Old Tom and dry, also available oaked) and 77 Whiskey (Local Rye Corn, New York Wheat)

Brooklyn Gin (brooklyngin. com): excellent, dry-style gin, founded by Joe Santos

Doc Herson's (doschersons. com): absinthes, made by husband and wife team Kevin Herson and Stacey Luckow

Greenhook Ginsmiths (greenhookgin.com): Gins— American Dry, Beach Plum (a local take on slow gin) and aged Old Tom, founded in Greenpoint, Brooklyn by brothers Steven and Philip DeAngelo

Jack From Brooklyn (jackfrombrooklyn.com): Sorel Liqueur, based on a Caribbean hibiscus liqueur recipe

Kings County Distillery (kingscountydistillery.com):

whiskeys made in Williamsburg, Brooklyn in a variety of styles—white whiskey, bourbon, peated bourbon, single malt and even an addictive chocolate whiskey.

NY Distilling Company (see page 334): Dorothy Parker Gin, Perry's Tot Navy Strength Gin, Chief Gowanus, Mister Katz's Rock & Rye, Ragtime Rye

The Noble Experiment (owneys.com): Owney's Rum, a white rum made in Bushwick, Brooklyn named after a Prohibition era mobster/rum runner, made by Bridget Firtle

Van Brunt Stillhouse (vanbruntstillhouse.com): Whiskey (American, bourbon, rye and single malt), rum and grappa made in Red Hook, Brooklyn

Notable Spirits Made in New York State

Albany Distilling (albanydistilling.com): they make whiskey, but their Quackenhouse rum is the standout

Coppersea Distillery (coppersea.com): Hudson Valley whiskeys made using old school distillation methods

Delaware Phoenix Distillery (delawarephoenix.com): located in Walton, a line of superb whiskey and absinthe founded by distiller Cheryl Lins

Nahmias et Fils (baronnahmias.com): Mahia (a superb, unaged fig brandy), rye whiskey and an apple brandy

Hillrock Estate Distillery (hillrockdistillery.com): a high end line of whiskeys made with grains grown on site, under the direction of master distiller Dave Pickerell and winner of many awards, including double gold at the NY International Spirits Competition

Long Island Spirits (lispirits.com): liqueurs, vodka and well made whiskeys (produced under the Pine Barrens and Rough Rider labels)

Five & 20 Spirits and Brewing (fiveandtwenty.com): beer, whiskey and liqueurs produced in Westfield.

Orange County Distillery (orangecountydistillery.com): excellent gins and whiskey made with locally grown grains

Prohibition Distillery (prohibitiondistillery.com): hooch (vodka, gin and whiskey under the Bootlegger label) made like it's 1921!

Tuthilltown Spirits (tuthilltown. com): one of the pioneers in the NY state craft distilling movement, they're known for their whiskeys (sold in cute 375-ml "baby" bottles) in addition to gin, vodka and liqueurs

—Spotlight—
Allen Katz of
NY Distilling Company

79 Richardson Street
Brooklyn, NY 11211
(718) 412-0874
nydistilling.com

One look at Plymouth Gin's distillery, located in the middle of a city street, and Allen Katz knew he wanted to open his own urban distillery some day. He began his career working at a cooking school in Italy and had been a key figure at Slow Food USA before becoming the Director of Mixology and Education with Southern Wine and Spirits. These experiences put him at the center of the burgeoning craft cocktail community, hobnobbing with all the rising stars. "Experimenting with Daiquiri ratios was still a new concept back then," he says. He was perfectly situated for the project.

By the time Katz and his partners Tom and Bill Potter began conceiving of NY Distilling Company, which opened in 2011, NYC liquor laws had begun allowing on-premise tastings rooms. The industrial space in Williamsburg, Brooklyn was perfectly set up to have two entrances, ideal for building a separate bar (the Shanty) overlooking the distillery.

The concept was always to create spirits (mainly gin and rye) specifically for craft cocktails—"purposeful products that stand along mainstream brands." They didn't want to release young whiskey aged in microbarrels, as so many other new craft distilleries do, in order to quickly turn a profit; instead, they laid down their rye in proper 53-gallon casks. And while it got its beauty sleep, they released two wildly successful New York City gins—the Dorothy Parker and Perry's Tot, a navy-strength gin named after a former Commandant of the Brooklyn Navy Yard. While the majority of the rye continued aging, they released some of the young rye in two unique spirits: Chief Gowanus, a rye-based Holland gin recipe made with the consultation of local drinks historian David Wondrich (see page 58); and Mr. Katz's Rock & Rye, which reimagines what many consider to be a cloying old-man drink into one with finesse, using sour cherry, citrus, cinnamon and even rock candy sugar. By the time Ragtime Rye was released after three years, a loyal NY Distilling Co. fanbase welcomed it with open arms.

New York Cocktails Elsewhere

Where to Get Back In the New York Groove Outside the City

Hop Sing Laundromat

1029 Race Street

Philadelphia, PA 19107

hopsinglaundromat.com

PDT + Laundromat + Philly = Hop Sing Laundromat.

Bryant's Cocktail Lounge

1579 S 9th Street

Milwaukee, WI 53204

(414) 383-2620

bryantscocktaillounge.com

Milwaukee's oldest cocktail lounge has been hip since it opened in 1938. There's no menu, per se (the original owner felt it was too limiting), but almost anything in the cocktail canon can be conjured from fresh ingredients and a variety of spirits. The only criteria is that guests stay open-minded., which is a very New York way to be.

Foreign National

300 East Pike Street

Seattle, WA 98122

foreignnationalbar.com

This Capitol Hill cocktail lounge set out to create a certain mood—the sort one can only experience in a sparsely lit room decorated with old world motifs. This is a very New York crowd; they want a cultivated drink menu, genial service and ambitious snack choices, and that's precisely what they get.

The Varnish

118 East 6th Street

Los Angeles, CA 90014

(213) 265-7089

Opened by Sasha Petraske, Eric Alperin and LA nightlife impresario Cedd Mosesand, this bar is hidden behind Cole's (originators of the French Dip). For obvious reasons, this little speakeasy-style joint is reminiscent of the old ones in New York. Its crowd and quiet energy also enhances the mood.

THE THREE CLUBS

1123 Vine Street
Los Angeles, CA 90038
(323) 462-6441
threeclubs.com

This bar has been in its Hollywood location since 1991, but a few years ago, it was resuscitated by Michael Neff—the "neighborhood bar whisperer"—who is partially responsible for breathing new life into New York's Rum House and Holiday Cocktail Lounge. It's also a cabaret and burlesque lounge; sadly, good cocktails and live music are a rare bird in NYC these days. As a bar, it has that edgy-but-elegant grit of the East Village, with friendly bartenders and a well-stocked bar.

THE MANIFEST

32 N. Hotel Street
Honolulu, HI 96817
manifesthawaii.com

Amid the palm trees and coconuts you'll find this Chinatown cocktail lounge in Oahu. High ceilings and brick walls are straight out of a Manhattan courtyard—but with better weather. Drinks like Day After Amaro solidify the experience.

BAR CHEF

472 Queen Street
Toronto, ON M5V 2B2
Phone: +1 416-868-4800
barcheftoronto.com

Dim lighting—check! Craft cocktails—check! 5,000 ounces of homemade bitters . . .well, if a New York bar could hold that many . . .

HARRY'S NEW YORK BAR

5 Rue Daunou, 75002 Paris
phone: 01 42 61 71 14
harrysbar.fr

The bar is a true Paris institution, inhabiting the same building in the 2nd arrondissement since 1911. As the story goes, it moved from New York to Paris, where it was subsequently bought by its first bartender, Harry MacElhone. This is where the Bloody Mary was invented before being brought back to New York's St. Regis Hotel (where it was renamed the Snapper). The atmosphere is a time capsule of NYC's jazzy era of nightclubs and cocktails. It's not only New York elsewhere, it's New York yesteryear.

Glass Bar

7 Rue Frochot, 75009 Paris
Phone: 09 80 72 98 83
glassparis.com

Glass was opened by the team behind Candelaria. Says nightlife photographer Gabi Porter, "It's open late, it's dark, they serve hot dogs, it's usually full of expats and bartenders and they have an unusually large American whiskey selection."

Scarfe's Bar at the Rosewood

Rosewood London
252 High Holborn
London WC1V 7EN
Phone: +44 20 3747 8611

The Campbell Apartment might be finished, but this London hotel bar is the next best thing. Step inside its handsome drawing room and sink into a plush seat by the fire, or saddle up to the long, elegant bar to forget your troubles.

Happiness Forgets

8-9 Hoxton Square
London N1 6NU
happinessforgets.com

Something about stepping down into this low-lit, laid-back bar in Shoreditch gave me the sense that I was walking into a Manhattan bar. Many London bars insist on some sort of theme these days, and I fully enjoy that, but I appreciate that this bar presents itself simply as a solid neighborhood cocktail bar.

Thelonious Bar

Weserstraße 202, 12047 Berlin
Phone: 49 30 55618232

The chic Neukölln neighborhood in Berlin boasts many cute bars, but this cocktail bar stands out for its relaxed, dark and jazzy (as the name suggests) atmosphere—with very sociable bartenders, to boot.

Jerry Thomas Project

Vicolo Cellini, 30
00186 Roma
phone: +39 06 9684 5937
jerrythomasproject.it

To be honest, JTP is really nothing like a New York bar experience. One needs a membership to drink there, and you can't even take photos inside (New Yorkers love to show people what they drink). However, the whole idea behind the bar is a speakeasy-adjacent; it's a version of a place 19th-century New York bartender Jerry Thomas would have wanted to work, though they're stocked with more eclectic spirits than he ever could have imagined. It's effectively a New York if the speakeasy trend had been taken to the next level.

Manhattan at the Regent, Singapore
1 Cuscaden Road, Regent Hotel
Singapore 249715
Phone: +65 6725 3377

Manhattan is a throwback to old New York sophistication, with classic cocktails to match. With many of the grand hotel bars of the city long departed, this is a taste of a forgotten tone.

Door 74
Reguliersdwarsstraat 74I, 1017 BN Amsterdam
Phone: 31 6 34045122
Door-74.com

This small cocktail bar in the central part of town feels like the lovechild of Milk Honey and Wallflower (the intimate West Village bar co-owned by bartender Xavier Herit). It's personable and lively, with a crowd to match. The cocktails created by bar manager Timo Janse and bartender Tess Posthumus are nothing short of exquisite.

Bar Tonique
820 N. Rampart Street
New Orleans, LA 70116
(504) 324-6045
bartonique.com

There are oceans of terrific cocktail bars in New Orleans, both old and new, and they are all distinctly New Orleans (in a good way). But on late nights, Bar Tonique transmits a serene air a couple of paces removed from the pulse of the city—much the way a good Brooklyn bar can exist in its own axis.

Of course, nothing anywhere can quite compare to sipping a cocktail while experiencing a quintessential New York moment. Businesses will close, people will move, staff will quit, relationships will end, but this magnificent ghost town will never sleep. Cheers to you, New York!

— Acknowledgements—

I would first like to thank Carlo DeVito for introducing me to John Whalen and the team at Cider Mill Press. I am extremely honored that Carlo had faith in me to bring this book to life. That wouldn't have happened if he hadn't found me through Alcohol Professor. Another huge thanks goes to Adam Levy, who has given me a platform to report the booze news in my own way. On that note—massive thanks to the growing number of readers who "get" us. And all of our writers who stepped up during this writing process and complete our boozy world.

I can't thank my dear friend Francine Cohen enough for her listening skills, sage advice and assistance in helping me make some much needed connections for this book and beyond. Thank you to Rachel Harrison for being awesome. To Stephanie Moreno for believing in me from the very beginning, sticking by through and through and late night palate cleanser texting sessions. To Jared Brown for his trusted friendship, gift of gab, time and guidance. Thanks to everyone who generously contributed their delicious recipes and photos in such a short turn-around, and to those who took the time out of their hectic schedules to speak with me and offer their wisdom, particularly David Wondrich.

A massive thank you to the supremely talented New York City drinks industry for continuing to delight and impress, to those who welcome us all into their spectacular watering holes (after all, a true sign of hospitality is making someone feel at home when you wish they were) and to all those who have left their mark on the world.

Thank you to my brother-once-removed Jason Bylan for being such a committed patron of the arts and such a fun boozy events date. Thank you to my dear friend John Hedigan—for your constant faith and devotion, and for not freaking out over my death-defying mood swings over the past few months.

Speaking of faith, no two people have shown more in me than my parents, Carlotta and David Schuster. Thanks for your enduring support of my crazy career. And for my first drops of Scotch, from a glass accidentally left on the living room table during a party when I was two. ("Mmmmm Scotch juice!") (I kid. My parents have incredible taste and I'm so thankful they have shared so many flavorsome adventures with me throughout my whole life.) Last but never least, thank you to my cat Jasper for making sure I took writing breaks and getting me up in the morning with his patented Pete-Townshend-windmill-paw-nose-honk.

—Index—

— Image Credits —

Photos by Amanda Schuster: pages 4, 5, 10, 16 (Gibson), 54-55, 70, 90, 94, 99, 101, 103 (bar), 129 (bar photos), 131, 197, 198-199, 224, 237, 323, 342, 350; pages 14, 44, 81, 82 courtesy of '21' Club; pages 39, 114, 117, 118 courtesy of Death & Co; pages 296-7, 334-5 courtesy of New York Distilling Co.; pages 19, 27, 109, 238, 251, 257, 260, 309 courtesy of Al Rodriguez Photography; page 21 courtesy of Jill DeGroff; page 24 courtesy of Jonathan Stas; page 30 courtesy of Clover Club; page 33 courtesy of Garret Smith; pages 36 and 53 courtesy of Pegu Club; page 40 courtesy of Giuseppe González; pages 41 and 155 courtesy of Tim Becker; pages 50 and 291 courtesy of Bryan Teoh; pages 57 and 124 courtesy of Eryn Reece; pages 87 and 148 courtesy of Meaghan Dorman; page 88 courtesy of Angel's Share; page 93 courtesy of Mimi Burnham; page 102 courtesy of Ivy Mix; pages 105 and 106 courtesy of Nicole Franzen; page 120 (sign) courtesy of Pouring Ribbons; pages 120 (cocktail and Joaquín) and 122: courtesy of Eric Medsker; page 126 courtesy of Natalie B. Compton; page 129 (Sother Teague) courtesy of Kyle Ford; page 132 courtesy of Timothy Murray; page 133 courtesy of Fort Defiance; page 138 courtesy of Isaac Rosenthal; page 140 courtesy of Leo Sorel; page 142 courtesy of Darryl Chan; page 144 courtesy of Emilie Baltz; page 150: courtesy of Jayd Jackson; pages 152 and 277 courtesy of Oleg March; page 156 courtesy of Josh Mazza, 11C; page 158 courtesy of Masa Urushido; page 161 courtesy of Scott

Gordon Bleicher; page 162 courtesy of Nick Voderman; page 165 courtesy of Kenta Goto; pages 166, 172, 179, 220 courtesy of Andrew Kist; page 170 courtesy of Chaim Dauermann; pages 182, 186 (Empire Hotel photos), 190-1 courtesy of Hospitality Holdings; page 186 (Scenic view Bar 54) courtesy of Christopher Villano; page 189 courtesy of Melissa Ortiz; pages 194, 270 (right), 272-273 courtesy of Paul Wagtouicz; page 200 courtesy of Keith Allison; page 208 courtesy of Jessie Gibson; page 215 courtesy of Noah Fecks; pages 217-18 courtesy of Brendan Burke; page 222 courtesy of Alexandra Foley Photography; page 226 courtesy of T.J. Lynch; page 228 courtesy of Leyenda; page 231 courtesy of David Nurmi; page 242 courtesy of Stork Club Enterprises; page 245: courtesy of Zachary Sharaga; page 247 courtesy of Kathryn Yu; page 255 courtesy of Steve Freihon; page 268 courtesy of Charissa Fay; pages 270 (left) and 295 courtesy of Joey Wehner; page 271 courtesy of Jessie Gibson and Thirsty; page 279 courtesy of Mike Di Tota; page 280 courtesy of Brian Matthys; page 282 courtesy of Carly DeFelippo; page 284 courtesy of ROKC; pages 287-8 courtesy of Frankie Rodriguez; pages 292-3 courtesy of Michael Tulipan; page 294 courtesy of Rich Wade; page 300 courtesy of Adam Aleksander; pages 301 and 319 courtesy of Gabi Porter; page 305 courtesy of Aidan Grant; page 314 courtesy of Colleen Newvine Tebeau and John Tebeau; page 316 courtesy of J.W. Perkins; pages 176, 234, 321, 324, and 325 courtesy of Naomi Leslie Photography

All other photos used under license from Shutterstock.com

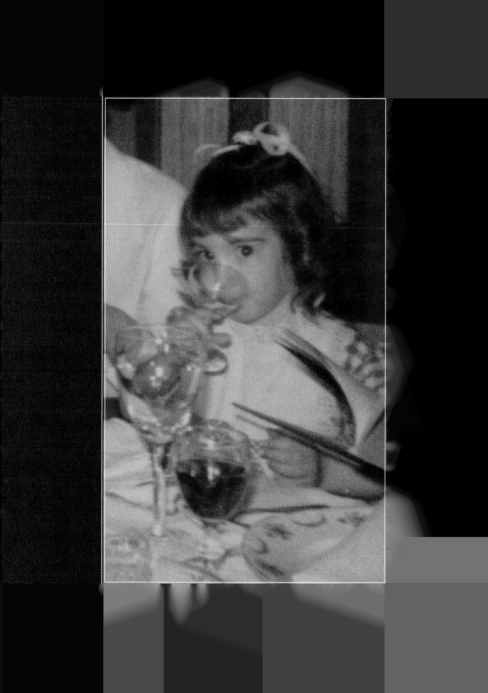

— ABOUT THE AUTHOR —

Amanda Schuster is a native New Yorker living in Brooklyn, New York. She is a freelance drinks, food and travel writer and Editor-in-Chief of the online publication Alcohol Professor. A classically trained pianist, medieval history major, photo researcher, jewelry designer and paper invitation specialist, she began a career in the alcohol arts in 2006 (one of her best friends once said she has "failed at more things most people have tried," which is a statement she wears proudly). Amanda has a certification from the American Sommelier Association and has since worked in the industry as a consultant, retail buyer, writer and marketer. As the Assistant Spirits Buyer of Astor Wines, she crossed into the world of stronger libations, where she learned to speak fluently in spirits and craft cocktails. She now considers herself bi-spiritual. For her, the exciting thing about the wine and spirits industry is that it's both traditional and ever-evolving. That's why, when asked which wine, spirit or cocktail is her favorite, her answer is usually, "The one I haven't tried yet." When she isn't writing, she likes to cook, travel, explore the city and its many restaurants, see plays and take in a good (or good-bad) movie.

—About Cider Mill Press Book Publishers—

Good ideas ripen with time. From seed to harvest, Cider Mill Press brings fine reading, information, and entertainment together between the covers of its creatively crafted books. Our Cider Mill bears fruit twice a year, publishing a new crop of titles each spring and fall.

CIDER MILL PRESS

BOOK PUBLISHERS

KENNEBUNKPORT, MAINE

"Where Good Books Are Ready for Press"

Visit us on the Web at
www.cidermillpress.com

or write to us at
PO Box 454
12 Spring St.
Kennebunkport, Maine 04046